Plateaus of Destiny

by Mike Gould

Illustrated by Mike Gould
Edited by Gary Hubbell

Clinetop Press
Post Office Box 95
Carbondale, Colorado 81623
970-963-0696 • 970-984-3801

ISBN #: 1-893740-00-5

It has been my custom for many years to enclose a feather in any correspondence with friends and family. They are equally beautiful to send as well as to receive. The feathers, however, are greatly significant. They are symbolic of real life issues, even wind direction, temperature, and attitude.

I have placed a feather on the cover of this book especially for you, the reader. It is a tail feather from a ruffed grouse. The complete tail fan represents a fullness of joy, an attitude of depth and reason. This feather is the fourth from the outer edge of the fan, on the right side of the bird.

It is a symbol of good tiding. I've never seen anyone who received one who didn't get a cozy, peaceful feeling about it. This feather represents a warm wind, probably a western, or Zephyr wind. It also indicates a certain degree of density, maybe even confusion. It will call you to look closer at your surroundings, to stay focused. Many times our lives resemble a pathway through thick timber in which we must be aware of every option so we can choose the right direction. The feathers at the outer edges of the fan have to make decisions quickly, often without much to go on. The ones in the center of the fan are accustomed to having decisions made for them. The feather I left for you is one of wisdom and understanding. It reminds you there is an abundance of knowledge awaiting those who exercise patience and diligence.

Yours with my warmest regards,

Mike Gould

Dedication

This book is dedicated to
Bryce, Jayme, Chelle, and Davey.

These are the arrows of my quiver, the arrows of my life.
Two have already felt the tension of the master's bow,
The others are patiently waiting.
Reach high for your answers, little souls,
for they are there at your reach.
Your every wish shall be granted,
for you are truly special and loved ones.
May your journeys be as beautiful as you are,
And as happy as you deserve.

Foreword

I should admit up front that I haven't known my friend Mike Gould very Long, nor even known *about* him until recently, and there is much to know.

For example, I had no idea of his status at being one of the best (if not *the* best) breeder and trainer of pointers and retrievers currently at work in the country (black Labs and Elhew pointers being his forte), until I had the unforgettable opportunity to work and photograph his efforts firsthand, but don't take my word for it. Mike has already been profiled and endorsed by the best field writers of the day for his techniques and innovations, and continues to be lauded for his efforts.

What he's asked me to do isn't quite as easy, at least to my mind. Mike has recently completed an incredible collection of stories; essays within essays really, of the journeys of a small-town kid to self-made man, though it's not as simple as that. Indeed, in Mike's own words, he describes his manuscript as "the life and times of a scrubby old dog trainer who enjoys few things better than to write about the should-have-been's, the could-uv's, and the Just-about's." Of course, it's not as simple as that either.

What *is* simple is that his stories are, well, simply wonderful: true, down-to-earth, easy-going refreshingly vivid. He writes in terms of reality: hard-luck times and coming to terms with one's limits; the deep, unspoken values of love, respect and friendship; the dreaming of dreams and the warmth and importance of a simple handshake. His stories are seriously considered and deeply felt.

Harry Middleton, author of a small but enlightening work called *"Rivers of Memory,"* wrote, in his own self-effacing way, that "a friend of mine who is a 'real' writer told me once that he believes a lone coyote howls in the deep of night because it seeks contact, connection, the company of other coyotes. Human beings, he went on to tell me, yearn for much the same thing. He said his books were nothing more than his own howls..."

Maybe.

In Mike's book, entitled "Plateaus of Destiny," you will find more than his own howlings, his own efforts at "contact and connection." You will find a clarity of observation in the tribulations of life that can make you step back and look at your own. What I quickly discovered in Mike's stories, in his reminiscences, were simple threads of life that bound it together, that made it make sense, that made it worthwhile. Not only in my life but the lives of those around me. Things that had been pushed aside and forgotten in the rush of our own struggles for purpose.

This is not a "how-to" book, of course, it's just damn fine writing; able to make you cry, to dream, and even to chuckle—and often. In "Sally and the Colonel," one of my personal favorites, Mike writes "I needed a good run, I'd been banged up pretty bad while trying to do business with some rich folks and needed to heal up some. Under the auspices of doing good business, that crowd routinely lays waste to honest, hard-working people without missing a bite of lunch..."

There are lessons to be learned too (or at least common sense to be reminded of). Also in "Sally and the Colonel," "You see, if you really want to know about a ranch, don't talk to a hired-gun biologist, talk to the guy who fenced it. If you want to learn everything about the water on the outfit, don't go to the water commissioner, talk to the guy who irrigated it. If his job depended on how much hay he put up, he learned how to get it wet...*all* of it."

Finally, in his recently completed "The Canyon of No Return," Mike writes, "Truth is forever on the wind...but its exact location is often concealed and almost always comes as a complete surprise. Sound familiar, my friend?"

Mike is a natural storyteller, something that's important in this hectic day and age. His style is good-natured, colorful and true, even riveting, if that's not too harsh a word. And what he's accomplished in "Plateaus of Destiny" is nothing short of what he's accomplished in his efforts and contributions to the dog-training world: damn near miraculous.

Finally, as you will discover, Mike has gone through his share of tough times recently, tough enough to make just about anyone else "lay down and cash it in." Yet Mike is grateful of the memories and thankful for what he has. We should be grateful too that during times when the will can side-step and stutter, he found the will to share with us his special spirit, and the spirit of the world that is home to us all.

Bruce Keep
Eagle, Colorado • April 15, 1998

Introduction

"Plateaus of Destiny" is a collection of true stories that both document and highlight certain plateaus along the journey of my life. This journey has been odyssean in nature, to say the least, and some time ago it occurred to me there are those who may enjoy reading about it.

Success, for all of us, seems to be more of an individual perception than anything else, and I've never known anyone who could accurately define it. It bears noting how a small-town boy, raised in the virtual obscurity of the Colorado Rockies, could have experienced those things written about in this book.

From childhood, I've enjoyed the honor of accompanying thousands of people to the field from every walk of life imaginable. I've walked with foreign royalty, dignitaries, celebrities, and sports stars; with top military brass, judges, corporate genius and billionaires. I've shared endless horizons with lawyers, doctors, construction workers, musicians, writers, and teachers. I've been educated in shade and sun by investment bankers, developers, architects, and Native Americans.

I've been lucky enough to benefit from the philosophy of life's unfortunate who sleep under bridges, in home-made tents, or in abandoned vehicles. I've been inspired by the wonder in the eyes of illegal aliens as they spend their first evening in the land of the free. I've shared my daily portion with them, and they with me. From the highest of the high to the lowest of the low, it's been quite a trip, my friend, quite a trip indeed.

The story of the people along the trail was enlightening for sure, but not more significant than the contribution of the wildlife and the boundless natural resources. I've worked 3,500 dogs and released over 100,000 game birds on ranches all over the western United States. I've personally guided 2,850 hunts and organized another 10,000 that were handled by trainer friends of mine.

My endless search for true meaning is much like a spider's web in appearance. In order to learn as much as I could about shooting dogs I was prompted to study birds. In order to learn of the birds I had to study habitat, food sources, and predators. This took me to animals, soil, water, fish, and insects.

Somewhere along the way I was engulfed in a dream that could never end.

As you follow through the pages, I hope you have cause to dream of the special people and places of your life. I hope the stories take you away into vivid memory of time gone by before they bring you safely home again. If you let them process in your heart, we'll have plenty to talk about when we meet a little further down the road.

Until then I leave with you my best regards,

Mike Gould

Table of Contents

Grouse Omen

My eyes snapped open. In the gray pre-dawn light the wind is cold and persistent. The wind always blows some along the Deep Creek Rim. In many places it breaks straight off and seemingly stuffs timber and rockslides into the canyon. From the edge, you can usually hear the creek rushing several thousand feet below. In some spots, it is visible in the moonlight as it quickly darts between thick stands of water-loving Douglas fir. The trees lean against the canyon wall, the crowns no further from the rock than the lower-most boughs.

There is something greatly mystical about looking out from a cliff; feelings of awe, feelings of fear, and feelings of happiness all take turns. You might feel secure, but at the same time anxious. You feel on top of the world as you look out upon the mountains, then utterly inferior when you look to the sky.

This mountain is one of many alpine plateaus and drainages that stretch back into the wilderness. At over 10,000 feet, this region is part of what is commonly known as the Montane, or Canadian Zone. Expansive mesas and radical topographical relief characterize this once-favored hunting ground of the Ute Indian Nation.

Much of the forest is very old up here. Logging camp ghosts and many young evergreens are entrusted to guard the old gray stumps until they finally crumble and fall to earth. Even while they sleep, the grand old Englemann spruce will nourish their progeny.

Oft times I walk through these woods. Although young trees give protection and offer camouflage, one can still visualize the forest as it once was. This is not a scene of death and sadness, but one of hope and celebration. The renewal of a forest is truly a wondrous thing to behold.

Rich, fescue-laden parks sprawl for miles along the canyon rims without appreciable change in elevation, while other parks look more like a blanket thrown over the woodpile. Quick drops and benches reveal pockets of quakies, willowy springs, and grassy meadows.

Sub-alpine shrubbery like serviceberry, chokecherry, snowberry, mountain mahogany, and Gambel oak reach into alpine draws until they become stunted and unproductive. The parks themselves are a spectacular setting of tall fescue and brome grass, complemented by virtually every wildflower species imaginable.

It is a particularly fine thing to watch storm systems move into these mountains and valleys. Sometimes they are moody. Raging in behind ominous black clouds, they throw their charges at the ground, then angrily exit amidst swirling, churning winds. These volatile storms are usually short-lived, but they often incite bad judgement and poor decisions. They are very reminiscent of the hardships of life that seem to descend on each of us without any noticeable warning. Our first reaction is to seek immediate relief, wherein lies the danger of choosing the first direction that looks attractive. Anyone who has been caught away from comfortable surroundings by the violent storms of life should think deeply about simply "holing up" until the sun breaks through again. The light that shines through directly following your dilemma is both rich and glorious. The trail that will lead you to safety will suddenly be obvious, where moments before, fear and desperation seemed to grip your senses.

Occasionally a storm settles in gently over the mountains and slips down into the valley like an arm around the shoulder of an old friend. This is a quiet storm that may stay on for a while, but most folks don't mind because this is the one that brings moisture, calms your spirit, and causes you to search inward. Again, the soft moisture is representative of quality counsel. You don't feel the urgency to get out of the weather, actually it's kind of nice just to stand out in it and absorb the true meaning. These extended circumstances will allow you to lay up wisdom and understanding... the unmistakable treasure of life.

Importantly, watching the weather patterns on neighboring mountains helps me plan my day. Nature almost always gives you time to get where you need to be before the storm, if you recognize and don't ignore her signs.

The alpine sights and sounds are accompanied by a complete array of scents to understand and unravel. Some are bold and seem to stand out above the others, but universal truths tell us there are riches below the surface, more subtle, but possibly greater.

These complex scents tell us of the condition of the mountain, what types of animals live there, and where they are. For example, for a long time I thought I could smell grouse. Later I realized I was actually smelling habitat.

I learned to equate certain smells with coveys. Sage, willow and wild licorice have a very distinctive odor. Elderberry, mountain ash, and cow parsnip carry heavy scents, especially when wet. Grouse love springs, as do many water-tolerant plants. These plants are often fresh with scent no matter what the conditions of the rest of the mountain. If you're in grouse country, and you smell this combination of habitat, your chances of seeing them are excellent. If you feel like working your dog, this would be a good place to start.

...I've come to accept
the long, languid grace of
the harrier as part of the
picture, a natural face
of the parks.
I've seen them slowly
cresting and gliding
above the ground,
A dignified application of
conservation and reason.

At daylight the grouse are feeding in the parks, and because of that, I try to be there also. It's always a little cold at first, but gradually I get lost in the glory of what I'm doing. The cooler temperature extends the endurance of both dog and man and usually enhances scenting conditions.

I've seen many young dogs—and a few people—learn their trade up here. I've watched as clumsy puppies grew into fabulous athletes. I've seen them come from jumping at flowers and chasing Mormon crickets into full-blown bird dogs, slashing the parks to ribbons. I used to think I brought them up here every year to develop their natural talents and to prepare them for the season. Now I know it is they who bring me up here each year, to give me a chance to develop my natural abilities and to prepare me for things to come.

Somewhere along the way, I learned of an Omen. The great Manitou, or spirit, of the Utes sent me a helper that took the form of a harrier, the long-winged hawk with the distinctive white patch above his tail. For years I've come to accept the long, languid grace of the harrier as part of the picture, a natural face of the parks. I've seen them slowly cresting and gliding just above the ground, a dignified application of conservation and reason.

Though I've seen ample evidence of grouse kills made by redtails and goshawks, the harrier always seemed content to stalk the bountiful cricket and rodent populations. I've never witnessed the taking of a grouse by a harrier. Why, then, was he always above prime grouse cover?

Were the harrier and the grouse occupying the same hunting ground in competition for the same food, namely Mormon crickets and grasshoppers? Were the grouse stirring rodents to the surface with their walking, scratching, dusting style of life? If that was the case, were they hunting in concert, each benefiting from the other?

Sometimes after carefully working an entire park, I'd tend to my dogs while the Omen called me back, circling over ground that I may not have covered. Had I missed the birds? Was he inviting me to look again, but closer this time?

The harrier has become special in my life because he has inspired me to wonder. Manitou has shared this great truth with me, and there must be others, many others, that go over an uneducated head.

Daybreak suddenly sprawled across the parks of the Flattops, providing glorious definition to what was, just seconds before, merely grayness in the foreground and silhouettes in the background. Five mountain ranges settled above the mist of the Eagle, Colorado, Frying Pan and Roaring Fork River valleys. The 14,000-foot peaks of the Continental Divide cut the sunlight into uneven rays as they sweep across the Western Slope of the Colorado Rockies.

I was standing beneath the oldest living thing in the Eagle District of the White River National Forest, a limber pine who holds the memory of at least 700 grouse seasons within her boughs. She is holding on, with a handful of others, along the southern rim of the Deep Creek Canyon.

Even though it was August, I zipped my jacket to the collar and slipped into my gloves. My fire seemed uncertain about its future as I neglected to stoke it while I stood and stared. Looking to the east, I tried to make out the Colorado River some 4,000 feet below. I knew roughly where it was, but it will be some time still before sunlight reaches those waters.

For now the morning seemed to be mine. I watched as the new day slipped along the granite face of the rim toward me until I was suddenly backlit and instantly warmer. Funny, I hadn't noticed a fairly hard frost. Soon the grass would be wet, and soon after would sway in the wind, dry and brittle.

I dipped half-a-pot of spring water and dropped a handful of coffee into my fire-blackened coffeepot. I twisted it carefully as I set it in the coals so it wouldn't tip or spill when I stirred my fire.

Today would be my last here on the rim. In the evening I would be moving up to my camp at the head of Coyote Park. That camp is settled just inside the timber at 10,640 feet. I favor that campsite for several reasons; I can drop into Grizzly Creek, Crane Park, Deep Creek, or Dead Horse Mountain no matter what kind of weather moves in. Even if I get caught in an early snowstorm, I can still get out by simply going downhill.

I am particularly fond of the violent thunderstorms that frequently skip across the ridge where I camp. Many lightning-struck Englemann spruce are strung from just below my camp on up north for several miles. Those huge old trees are twisted and charred by the events of their undoing. Some of them seem to have grimaced as they crashed to the ground and are frowning still where they lay. By walking slowly through these woods and studying the story left behind, one can understand why I have named this place, "The Woods of Many Faces."

I have witnessed some astonishing feats of lightning and thunder while standing under my tarp. I like to stretch it tight between four lodgepole pines so it will turn the rain and keep most of my stuff dry. Many days my dogs and I have held fast and peered out while sizzling strikes singled out unlucky victims. The lightning awakens every sense within my spirit, and the immediate thunderclap is so deafening, I sometimes fear the sky is tearing apart.

I recall stories I've heard about self-made men. I hear how they achieved fame and success on their way to the top by their own determination and perseverance. I hear how they have reached their crowning glory as a result of their own individual effort.

I wonder if he knows anything about true power,
This self-made man.
I wonder if he knows
he has been the
benefactor of grace, and
redemption.
I wonder if he's ever seen
lightning strike a tree?

You know, the Bible often compares the lives of men to that of trees. God's own word teaches us to aspire to be as trees, our foundations firmly rooted near rivers of living

water... rivers flowing with his spirit of truth.

I wonder if he has ever seen true power, this self-made man. I wonder if he realizes he has been the benefactor of grace and redemption. His humility may be hopelessly buried, his heart may not be able to speak... I wonder if he's ever seen lightning strike a tree.

My thoughts were suddenly interrupted by my fire as he hissed his disapproval of the coffee boiling into the coals. I quickly reached into the steam and snagged the bail with a custom hook. I grinned as I set the pot on a flat rock next to the fire. Tooter Shanklin taught me how to make that hook over thirty years ago.

Tooter was from west Texas. For many years he hunted mule deer with my dad over on Cottonwood Pass. His easy Southern manner made him a favorite around camp. I turned to look. I could just make out the aspen-covered mesas of Cottonwood Pass even though it was at least thirty miles from where I was standing. Between us was the sheer grandeur of the Glenwood Canyon and the hazy, swirling mist rising off the whitewater of the Colorado River.

I squinted into the morning and slowly skimmed my eyes along the distant mesa until I settled on familiar landmarks. I knew where the trail comes off the top and lowers itself into a dense patch of quakies at the edge of Spring Park. "That was Dad's camp," I said out loud.

It was not only my dad's hunting camp, it was where Tooter showed me how to make the hook I had just used to rescue my coffee out of the fire. It is an easy thing to close my eyes and visualize some of the great bucks that were hung to cool in those quakies while we laughed around another fire of another time.

I looked at the ground and continued to reminisce. It is also in that camp my dad told me he was dying. I saw him standing behind one of the tents by himself one morning. I don't know if he knew I was walking toward him and I don't know if he wanted me to see him as he rubbed the inside of his right arm. He was trying to relieve the symptoms of his heart disease. He had placed a nitroglycerine pill under his tongue and was rubbing his arm in an effort to work out of the chest pain that continued to plague him. I had seen him go through the same procedure on many occasions and offered to rub his arm for him. I enjoyed doing it; it made me feel like I was helping somehow.

"This'll be my last trip," he said almost casually.

"What do you mean, Dad?" I wasn't sure if I wanted to hear what he had to say.

"I won't be able to make it to any more hunting camps, kid. I think it's the end of the line for me."

"Aw, heck, Dad, you'll be all right. It's just awful cold out here this mornin'. Let's head over by the fire." I was swallowing hard on a lump that wouldn't budge. He looked away for a while, then looked back to me. "I don't want to go over there until the pain stops. I don't want everybody worried about me up here."

A month and a half later my dad died as he lay in my arms at home. Thirty-two years later I've still got the lump, and I've still got Tooter's hook.

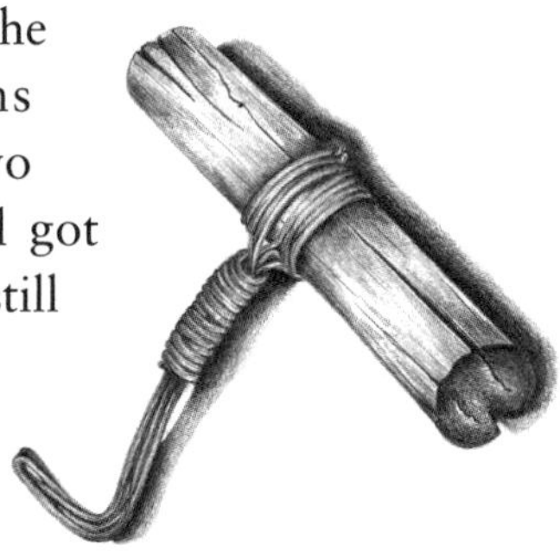

Tooter's hook
was hard to beat,
But a guy should
not aspire.
For there's nothing
quite like
god's own hand,
To pull treasure
from the fire.

By now I'd worried a sizable scrub in the ground with the toe of my boot, but I wasn't moving until I finish my coffee.

"Thank you, Father," I said. Again, I was talking out loud to myself, thanking my natural father for first taking me to the mountains, and also thanking my Heavenly Father for allowing me to learn of their value.

The dog box rattled as six pointers stretched and tapped the sides of the box with their firm tails. They were yawning as they tested creaky, stiff muscles and pushed against foot pads to check their running gear. I opened the box, cushioned their drop to the ground, and snapped them, one by one, to the chain gang.

For a short time they bristled and stood erect even though they had been sleeping together all night. Pointers are funny that way. They always like to establish some ground rules as quickly as they can. This team had been raised together, so there was never any fighting, just posturing and bragging. Their tails were wagging as they shook off the last of their bedding. I filled a water bucket and started down the line.

I like to talk to each of them and touch them while they're drinking. "Oh, you're not so tough, how's your shoulder this morning?" I looked down the line at one young male who was standing up on his back feet, pawing the air. "What are you so fired up about? I'll be down there in a minute. By the way, you better play better today, or I'm sending you down to the B team for a while." There's something to say to each of them as they drink and lift their heads to say hello.

"There's grouse in those parks, and it's our job to find them, so we might as well get started. Who's ready to get the ball rolling?"

I unsnapped a pair of white-and-orange pointers and asked them to stand while I checked my fire and grabbed my shotgun off the dog box.

"Let's go," I said, and stood there a moment to enjoy the competition as they both sprinted to the front. The dogs on the chain gang were hollering, "Hey, what about us?" I walked out of camp. They knew I'd be back for them before long. Boy, what a job, I can walk to work, no traffic or crowds, and I have the best workmates imaginable.

I was already digging for my sunglasses. I can't believe how quickly the day comes on once it finally gets going. As the light hit the park, the ground seemed to open up in front of me. This thing must be at least a thousand acres. Hoar frost jewelry still dangled from waist-high fescue heads and high-country flower arrangements were dazzling in crystal.

Splashes of white were streaking across the park—the dogs were flying. They were reaching for the skyline as I started to get into the workout. At this time they were running flat-out, but not hunting all that well. It would take them a minute or two before they settled into their working gait and concentrated on business.

The first covey broke into three pieces as the dogs blasted through the scent cone and pulled up to watch the birds disappear. No need in me correcting them, the lesson was at hand. Within five minutes they were leaning into the second covey, showing their very best bird-handling style.

"That's more like it," I kidded them. "I was beginning to think you guys couldn't find a pork chop in a phone booth."

By 10 a.m. I logged in 8 coveys and 61 grouse. I was sitting on a big rock watching the last pair of dogs cut up the area between two patches of quakies surrounding a pretty seeping spring.

I have to admit, I wasn't paying attention. I was dreaming and drifting as I crumbled wild licorice seeds in my fingers and breathed in the familiar fragrance. Sometimes I drop it into my coffee. I can't decide whether I like the taste or not, but just doing it makes me feel better.

I saw three mule deer hustle out of the quakies with both of my dogs in hot pursuit. Dang, I should have been ready for that. I hopped off the rock and circled enough to gain their ear. "Come on, now, it's getting so I can't take you anywhere." I acted a little upset while I walked them back toward camp, but who was I kidding, they've had just as good a morning as I have.

The lunchtime air was warm and very still. It is not uncommon for the temperature to range over 60 degrees within the course of a single day up here. Soon I was eating a fried grouse sandwich with one hand and poking the fire with the other. Occasionally I talked to the dogs, but I always talk to myself.

"You know, someday I'm going to write a book about working pointers, and if you stiffs are lucky, I'll put you in it. Do you think anyone would actually read about what we do up here? Most trainers are out there making a name for themselves on the classic field trial circuit, and I doubt if any of them would haul your sorry hides across the country.

"In the meantime, you found a pile of grouse this morning and I dusted a couple of them." The dogs weren't listening, or if they were, they pretended to be asleep. They groaned and snored as I propped my jacket against the base of the pine tree and layed down.

Off to the west I saw a harrier sailing low, hugging the ground. He was motionless with the exception of an occasional twitch of his long, barred tail feathers. "Oh, come on, now, don't give me that," I called to him. "We couldn't have missed much out there this morning."

He edged out over the canyon wall and was quickly swept into the heavens by rising thermals. "I'll see you tomorrow, buddy," I pledged. "Right now I'm going to take a nap."

This magnificient dog would often stand
While the hazy distance comsumed his stare,
It is my solitary wish to someday catch but a small glimpse
Of what he saw out there

The Legend of the Mountain Spirit

From the earliest times I remember, men have respected the mountains. My dad spent most of his time either hunting or fishing in the high country of Colorado.

As children, my siblings and I clung to the ragged edges of a pickup bed while Dad drug us from one mountain to another along creeks and up river valleys. We weren't usually prepared for the cold winds that whipped around the cab and stung our hands and faces. It didn't really matter. We stood up most of the time, leaning over the cab, pushing and laughing.

One November day we made a trip up on Cottonwood Pass to deliver supplies and help with hunting camp chores. Dad decided to haul several big mule deer bucks down off the mountain that afternoon. He waited in camp until all the hunters were in, so we could throw on any deer they had shot during the day. Sure enough, they brought in two nice four-points on towards evening. We quickly loaded them on top of the others and started on out.

We had a long drive in front of us. We had to cross the better half of Grand Mesa before dropping into Coulter Creek. Driving along the top would go slowly, and it would be long after dark before we would see the sparkles of Carbondale's town lights in the valley.

The men crowded into the front seat of the truck and slammed the door behind them. My sister, Hallie, and I jumped into the back and zipped up. We stood up there until dark, each looking hard to the edges of the parks. There were still licenses to fill and many big bucks were taken either going up or coming down from camp.

We continually brushed tears from the corners of our eyes and squinted to scan the scattered patches of quakies and big sagebrush. The men in front were looking, too, but it was a matter of pride. We wanted to see the deer first.

Gray light turned to darkness and the headlights came on out front. Dad stopped at the last gate and I bounced out to get it taken care of. You see, that was the other reason he brought us. There must have been twenty cobbled-up wire gates that had to be opened and closed on the way in or out.

This time my legs didn't have the usual spring when I hit the frozen road, and this time my cotton gloves stuck to the barbed wire when I tried to pry it off the gate post. It was getting cold.

My dad rolled his window down an inch or two and said, "You kids doin' okay back there?" Oh, yeah, like they were going to ask us to come up front. We knew as well as they did, there wasn't any room for us up there. As he pulled out onto the gravel county road and started picking up speed, Hallie and I looked at each other, then buried our faces in our jacket collars. It wasn't working. This was going to be one miserable ride to town.

I think we were both frantically thinking of a better plan. It came to us simultaneously when Hallie commented on how much those two bucks were still steaming. Within thirty seconds, she crawled into the body cavity of one, and not needing an invitation, I dived into the other. Not only did we stay warm the rest of the way home, we found the ride to be cushioned and soft. We both slept peacefully.

All of the families in our part of the country spent as much time as they could enjoying the mountain scenery. They probably had their favorite place. I know our family did—Basalt Mountain. I honestly can't say for sure if it was everyone's favorite, but it was certainly the most respected.

I've sat silent in the corner of the room while my dad traded hunting stories with friends and family. I noticed their looks would turn serious when Basalt Mountain was brought up. My grandpa, my Uncle Dick, my brother Bob, and my dad would suddenly grow quiet and gaze distant for a time. Occasionally one of them would walk over to the side window of our house and gaze out toward the dark, moody silhouette on the eastern skyline. I guess they were all thinking of their own special memory.

As I grew up, I learned to respect that mountain as well. I learned that every man who spent any time at all up there was secretly fearful of something he couldn't quite put his finger on. If a guy frequented Basalt Mountain and wouldn't own up to being seriously lost at least a couple of times, one of two things was happening: he was either spending most of his time sitting in his rig, or he was lying through his teeth.

The mountain itself is nothing special, really. It's only about 10,900 feet tall, with no great jagged cliffs or sagging canyons. No part of the mountain is actually above timberline, and the mountain is heavily forested. The lower reaches are covered by a mixture of sub-alpine shrubbery like sagebrush, Gambel's oak, serviceberry, chokecherry and mountain mahogany. Scattered patches of quaking aspens act as a transition zone between the shrubs and dense evergreen timber at the top. My dad called it "black timber." Rich combinations of alpine grass grew waist high in the parks and brilliant wildflowers yanked your head from one side to the other as you passed by.

My grandparents and parents homesteaded, worked and lived at the foot of the mountain. I think it must have been there, in those log cabins, my family was given the gift of the Mountain Spirit.

I would like to take you along on a spiritual trip, give you a glimpse of a memory or two, and introduce you to the Mountain Spirit. First, I'd like to tell you about him. The Mountain Spirit has a job. He's a maintenance man supreme. His job is to keep the mountain in balance.

Sometimes he has to make painful decisions, like burning off some timber, or washing a gully. He watches while people upset the balance of his work and he has to fight to hold everything together. The birds, the animals, the trees, the rocks, grasses and water are all his responsibility.

There is only one road that will take us from the valley floor, along Cattle Creek, to the top of Basalt Mountain. Though it doesn't look it, this is one of the most fierce jeep roads anyone could ever encounter. Here at the bottom, it isn't unlike any of the other four-wheel-drive roads in this part of the Rockies. It starts with a gentle sweep around a nice park sprinkled with many quakies—easy stuff for even a rookie four-wheeler. As the road quickly gets rougher, you may start to gain a sense of appreciation for the mountain's sense of humor.

It takes experience and some certain acquired skills to drive on that thick black clay, especially when it's wet. Mud puddles may look so innocent, but if you don't know how to handle them, the Mountain Spirit will have you before you get a quarter of the way up the hill. The trick is to ease into the puddle and then power on through before the muck factor can stop you dead.

The first few mudholes are there just to warm you up—you know, build your confidence. After barely spinning out of one, you make a mental note to hit the next one a little bit faster. How could you know there is a rock the size of a refrigerator lurking just 1/16 of an inch below the placid surface of the water? You take a tiny run at the puddle, then as you start to push on through, something underneath finds the rock. Just for a second you won't know what's happened, and your forward progress grinds to a halt as you let up afterward.

You see, the mountain knows how to cripple you. He knows he can knock off a mirror, scratch the paint, even break a window without even slowing you down. He sees your vehicle as a porcupine, with its one true weakness underneath. A flat tire is a delay at best, but a good blow to the transfer case can put you down for the count. Nevertheless, people were always tempting the Mountain Spirit. One time we came across a '57 Thunderbird up on the top of Basalt Mountain. The driver of that car could always say he made it, and it's true, we saw it. But the damage that

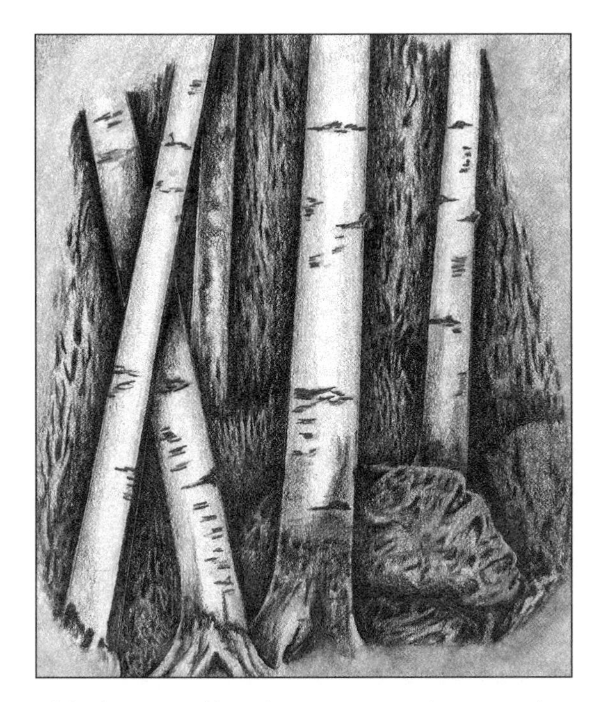

Granted, some trailheads are hard to distinguish, Thankfully, not all sign is equally difficult to read.

old classic suffered getting up there made you want to take your hat off. It was sure too bad.

Right after the first mudholes, as you come around the next corner, there's a little pullout in the quakies. Right there is where my cousin Walt and I caught the game warden poaching grouse one day. Our rig was broke down on top and we had to walk off the mountain. We were keeping to my grandpa's old logging skids so we didn't have to zig-zag through all the switchbacks. This was the same trail my dad worked from the time he was a baby. Grandpa would hitch a log to a workhorse and send him down out of there to the homestead miles below. Dad was ten years old.

Walt and I knew this was the quickest way down and we were both familiar with the signs along the old trail. We were making time, jogging where we could, and high-stepping it the rest of the way. We came out of the timber and skidded to a stop in time to see the game warden finish off a covey of blue grouse with his .22 pistol.

"Looks like I owe you one," he said as we hurried past.

"Looks like," we laughed.

Walt and I were a lot like brothers growing up. I remember

being lost with him at least once and share great memories of growing up together. One day, back on top of the mountain, we teamed up on a buck. Walt took a poke at him while he was standing in the timber, and, lo and behold, here he came, charging down that trail toward us like he meant business. I don't know if he was charging us, but it sure looked like it. Walt jumped off the trail one way and I went the other. When the deer ran past, I let him have it, right from the hip. He slammed into the ground between us.

After the dust cleared, Walt whispered, "I smell elk."

"Come on now, Walt," I said. "We're already lost, we just danged-near got run over by a buck, and now you smell elk."

We both stood there and checked the wind. Walt was right—it was elk for sure. We chased down a decent cow and Walt put the touch on her before we went about finding our way back to camp. That was my first time smelling elk, and I'll never forget it. Every time I smell them, I think of Walt.

At the next bend in the road, an old stove lies half-buried in the meadow grass. It doesn't look like much, but believe me, it's as big a part of this trip as anything you'll see today. That stove is one of our landmarks—it was lying there next to the road a long time before I was born. On the right there is the old government trail to High Park. You can't really see it anymore, but if you can find it, and then stay on it, it'll take you to the northern tip of the Park.

I shot the biggest mule deer buck of my life in the breaks below High Park. Later that same day I came across a tom cougar in a driving snowstorm. He was loping through sparse quakies and Douglas fir towards the lava beds of the rim. A guy has to learn to shoot at a target moving through timber if he's ever going to get much done in this country. My dad taught me those lessons, and I remembered them long enough for the cat to pay the price.

We packed that lion out in over two feet of snow.

High Park is extremely rough country. It was always best to hunt that country on horses, I figured. It was here that I realized that the mountain can be very dangerous. The mountain can hurt you and you should always take it seriously. Being alone in High Park as darkness sets in at the same time as a snowstorm can make you think about how prepared you are.

A small, gurgling spring emerges from the tip of High Park and skirts in and out of a long lava bed along its course. Finally it gains enough momentum to surface for good so you can see the pretty blue tint of the water. Willows and berries cluster at its banks where it rushes out of the woods onto a grassy little bench called Blue Creek Flats.

It was there at those flats where we parked our truck on September 12, 1961, and dropped a young German shorthaired pointer to the ground. It was grouse season. He casted away into the thickness of serviceberry, chokecherry and acorn-bearing brush. An hour later he surprised a pair of yearling bear and put them to tree. I was eleven years old, carrying a .22 rifle, and my first bear, shot three times, came crashing to the ground. My bird dog was courageous as the first bear tumbled from the tree, but the second sent him howling to the truck.

As we move on up the trail to the place where the quakies begin, I close my eyes and visualize a time when I saw Ralph Long coming through the golden trees at a full gallop. He was riding an Arabian gelding and leading two saddle horses, one in each hand. I had never seen horses running through the trees before. It was truly moving and beautiful. His hat was pulled down tight and he was smiling broadly. He was spurring and yelling and floating on his saddle.

All three horses were lathered and working as they each gathered and cleared a spruce deadfall together. Ralph was at home. The mountain embraced him. We had lost our horses while elk hunting and Ralph, knowing the horses and where our camp was located, had brought them all the way from Missouri Heights, some fifteen miles.

Now, as we crest the ridgeline, we are slowly inching through an unbelievable stretch of lava rock. First you have to ease one tire up on a rock, and then follow by raising another before the jeep drops off the first. It's a very interesting method of maneuvering through big rocks. The trick is to keep the oil pan and other vital parts of the vehicle from coming into contact with disaster. Actually, I like to drive through here. It's a good measure of a person's mountain driving skill. If you make it regularly, you're good. If you trash your rig, you're walking.

The spirit loves to sweeten the pot a little as you creep along from rock to rock. There are both wild raspberry and thimbleberries that grow just to either side of the road...and where there are berries, there are grouse. I often find myself driving through this section by feel alone, because my mind and my eyes are distracted by much more compelling interests.

At the top of the lava bed we will break out on top of a huge bench. It feels like the top of the mountain, but it's only false hope. There is much to come, only we will walk from here. Truthfully, it's faster than driving and a heck of a lot more comfortable.

We will stay on this bench as it bends around the mountain to the east. Piles of old sawdust will continually remind us of a time when loggers removed beetle-killed timber. This forest is so dense in places that a horse can't get through. I silently wonder how the elk ghost their way through the woods so easily. The timber is old and chaotic deadfalls are everywhere. Just to walk into this area is a truly fearful experience.

Most of the forest is made up of lodgepole pine, Douglas fir, and stunted blue spruce. The road is barely wide enough for a jeep. The obstacles are continually changing, and again, the joke is on you if you aren't prepared to move a rock or a fallen tree. It's not unusual at all to have to cut your way in, or out.

The trees here are always swaying and creaking, light is poor, and the only breaks in the timber are, unfortunately, the lava beds. Great mule deer bucks roam these reaches, but they have no interest in being seen or admired. A few elk keep them company but give them their room. The only will they heed is that of the Spirit. The only king the mountain has, or needs, is his spirit, and everyone knows it.

Coming up on the left is the Bear Waller. I know it's technically spelled "wallow," but not in this family. I've often caught glimpses of game along the edges of the waller, but every time I gave chase, the trail would take me to the dark north rim of the mountain before disappearing into the lava beds. "Too scary," I would think to myself. While going back to the waller, it's hard to fight of that "being watched" feeling. You know the one, the skin on the back of your neck seems to tingle and you feel like walking faster. You can't run—that would be unlike a child of the mountains—but you want to, for sure.

Just as the woods seem prepared to close in on us, I'm reminded of the time Uncle George lost his diamond ring. "It was right in here somewhere," he would always comment as we passed by. I can't remember ever really looking for it. What's a diamond ring worth out here, anyway?

See that old dead log over there? I once used it for protection while our hunters shot every bullet they had at a big bull elk. I'd been following him and about ten cows for about half a mile when we all came out into this park together. The hunters were where they were supposed to be and the elk came out where they were supposed to. The only problem was, somehow the elk were directly between the hunters and me. Hey, I had seen lots of elk, so I decided to wait the whole thing out while laying flat behind that log. Bullets make an odd hissing sound as they sing over your head, a sound I won't forget.

Even though the elk was wounded, he escaped the initial barrage and slipped into the timber. My sister ended up killing him as he tried to circle below us, through lava rocks the size of houses.

Let's stop to rest as soon as we get into these quakies. Right there, on that little knob, is where my dad sat waiting as I walked toward him with the heart of my first bull elk dangling from my hand. I had shot him earlier in the drive. My thoughts had been only of my dad, and what his reaction would be when I finally reached him. Even now I can see the smile on his face when he realized what had happened. He had killed a monster buck just minutes before, but gave me the glory.

How could I know I would never hunt elk with my dad again? I feel tears trickle down my cheeks, and a funny warmth as I remember the respect I have for him and the mountain he loved like no other.

This park we are now walking through is one we called the Heifer Pasture. It is here I saw the most dramatic event of my hunting lifetime. I was told to take my hunters to flank a long stretch of dark timber while my dad and brothers walked toward us. Before a drive can be successful, each party must hold up his end of the stick. Everyone has to be where they're supposed to be, and they have to be there at the right time. My grandpa had memorized the preferred escape routes that big bucks use when they are pressured. He learned to push them from one area while his hunters watched from another.

The bigger a buck gets, the fewer mistakes he makes. They are very proud and don't like to turn and run. They will generally bed where they can vacate the premises quickly and quietly. They won't bounce, like a younger buck or a doe. They favor a stiff-legged jog that both eats up ground and creates almost no sound.

A big timber buck has a very distinctive and different appearance than most mule deer. His body is blocky and square, his neck powerful and muscular. His legs look shorter than they should be and his manner is serious. His face shows more gray than the smaller bucks, and his nose is rounded, or "roman." His antlers are thick and very dark, sometimes lighter at the tips of the tines like a bull elk's. The base of the rack is as gnarly as a river bed, clustered with bumps and bulges that are never completely cleaned of velvet.

I can easily visualize this greatest of all big game animals as he came strutting out in front of us and jolted to a stop. He snorted and glared at us from 75 yards or so. My god, what a buck. His immense spread snatched our attention—six on a side. I'll never see a more perfect animal, except when I dream.

As we enter the timber, at the far end of the Heifer Pasture, we will come upon the remains of our old hunting camp. We stayed there for years during the hunting season. Parts of the pole corral still hold fast to their supports while the other ends are slowly being claimed by the earth that bore them.

I put aside my memories. It is here I will introduce you to the Mountain Spirit. Pull up a stump while I build a fire. He will verify my story and help us relax, as every fire before him. You can be assured, your life will never be the same.

The Mountain Spirit is not hard to find. I simply recognize his presence and formally ask approval of our intentions. We may have come for grouse, or a nice buck, but we will take what he gives us and go about our way. You see, he only allows us to come and go as he wishes. We are his guests. He runs this show from beginning to end.

The spirit tells me of a gift he has given you. He has asked me to explain it and I will do the best I can. The gift is in the form of a document. This document is very tiny. He has placed it in the furthermost corner of your heart. On the document is written the laws of this mountain. The laws tell of what is expected as you spend time here. From this time on, you will never take more than your share. You will never litter or deface the rocks or trees. You will always be careful with fire. You will forever realize the importance of addressing the spirit as you come. You will always be grateful, even though the spirit may deny your request. You will love these animals and birds as if they were your own.

You will try to understand the value of all involved, instead of just what concerns you. Catching a hundred fish is easy in these creeks—keeping only what you need is not.

The Spirit tells me the document is in your heart and so it is. You may leave it there and refuse its prompting, but it will always be there. When you abuse these laws, your heart will ache with unfamiliar pain. As you learn moderation in all your ways, the ache will turn to gladness and appreciation.

During this phase of your life, you will become more and more aware of the laws. You will begin to take pride in what you do, and maybe for the first time, be part of your surroundings.

As the phenomenon develops, the document will start to grow. It will continue to get larger according to your ability to absorb its meaning. There will come a day when the document will cover your entire heart, and still another when it fills your soul. As your mouth is the fountainhead by which your soul may speak, you will suddenly have the opportunity to give the gift of the Mountain Spirit to those around you. By telling others of your experience, you will place the document in the hearts of many.

Throw a couple of sticks on the fire, will you? Please don't be afraid of what I've said. Oh, yes, it's true. I don't have to describe the feelings you are feeling right now. You needn't be afraid of the Spirit, either. He has allowed us this day in his kingdom, and he has given you a great gift. The Mountain Spirit is a friendly one. I have known him all my life. He has given me many memories, a few of which I have shared with you today.

The Spirit is also a loving one, for I was born of it. The Spirit of this mountain is also the spirit of my father. I treasure the air I'm breathing right now.

Quietly we both stare into the fire. Maybe it makes sense, maybe it doesn't. The wind shuffles the tops of the pines ever so slightly, causing me to look up. I hear a distant elk call his challenge from somewhere down under the rim. I think he's right about where my grandpa's cabin used to be. The sign is clear enough, it's time to get going.

I didn't get to show you where I shot my first grouse, or my first deer. There is, however, one more thing I would like to do today, and it's starting to get late. Darkness seems so much more final in this timber. Have you noticed how long it is in coming and how short in going?

Will you help me? We must keep an eye out on our way, for I'm looking for a walking stick. Not just any stick will do. This one must come from a protected place. We must look for it in a leeward break from the wind. I will give it to a friend in need. He doesn't need anything fancy or glitzy—he's seen plenty of that in his day. He doesn't really even need a new one, for I know he has one that he brought home from Russia, from the mountain named Baba Dug.

The lingering cruelty of arthritis has left him in need of support. Support comes in many ways—some spiritual, some moral, and some physical. I need to find a sturdy stick, but not too heavy. You ask why it must come from a place out of the wind? Because he has felt enough wind in his day, both that he was making as well as that he was bracing himself against.

I will also look on the southern slope, for then I know the sun has warmed it as much as possible. This friend of mine is also in need of warmth these days. If you're wondering if I believe a walking stick can warm him, I answer that it's what he believes that counts. When modern medicine and technology can't warm him and bring relief to his legs, a walking stick sure as hell can't hurt.

There's one, you say. Nope, that one won't work, either. Why not? Because it's too young and springy to be a walking stick. A stick like that will bend when you need it most, just like some people. You need to pick a walking stick like you would choose a good friend—one that will be there when it's really needed.

Wait a minute. You know, there is one more place I would like to show you before we get to the jeep. C'mere and get up on top of these rocks. Take a look. Beautiful, isn't it?

That's the Roaring Fork Valley down there, and off to the east is where the Frying Pan River comes in. In between are the mountains that make up the Elk Range. Damn, you can see way above Aspen to the Continental Divide. The head of the range is a pair of 13,000-foot peaks called Mount Sopris. Some say it is the most photographed mountain in the world. I don't know how they could ever prove that, but it would be equally hard to disprove.

Off to the southwest of Sopris is Chair Mountain and the Ragged Mountain Range. The Crystal River cuts through the granite walls of the Redstone Canyon to the tiny town of Marble. Long before I was born, they brought marble out of there to fashion many national landmarks.

Off to the west, where the sky is churning up and bending light to form a sunset worth remembering, you can just make out the canyons of the Colorado River. See that little park below us? I remember once I saw a herd of elk sunning themselves along that bench.

Well, what do you know, there it is. There's the stick I'm looking for. Yep, that's it, not too fancy, not too heavy. Can you just imagine what this stick has seen in its lifetime? To spend a few passing minutes here is wonderful. To live here all your life...wow.

All the way down we ride in silence. We watch as the tiny mountain towns light up with nightfall. As we bump around Missouri Heights Reservoir, I wonder if you guessed that my family's homestead was on the other shore. I decided not to tell you. I figured you probably had enough used-to-be's and I-remembers.

I will take this time to thank the Lord for my life and the Mountain Spirit for our day together. And, oh yes, thanks for the walking stick, Daddy. As you well know, a good friend is hard to come by.

Though we are bound by family,
Bound by race.
We are single in spirit,
Single, by grace.

Though we are bound by our fury,
But free in the light.
With courage unfettered,
Boundless in flight.

Changes

I don't know what I was thinking as I sent two young pointers up the side of Willow Peak with the blackest storm clouds of the season bearing down on us from the west. I knew this was a big one—the thunderhead had been visible for two hours. I watched as it pummeled the Thompson Creek drainage forty miles to the south. I hoped it would stay to the south of Glenwood Canyon until it rammed into the taller mountains of the Divide. If I was lucky, I would catch some terrific winds for a time, but escape the fury of the electrical storm.

I stood under a drooping spruce tree and watched the skies while my dogs relaxed on a spongy bed of accumulated, decomposed needles. I kind of hate to let them lay beneath spruce trees because there is so much sap around them. It's just the nature of a spruce to produce lots of weeping, dripping pitch. It sticks to anything it touches and takes me forever to remove it from the dogs' hair. If I'm running Labs, I don't mind it that much, but it looks bad on the white pointers.

This storm was a dandy. It had just crossed the Roaring Fork Valley and was closing in on Lookout Mountain and Buck Point. My mind trailed to the Buck Point Ranch project I had worked on in the early Eighties. "That's one of the most beautiful ranches I've ever seen," I thought to myself. The owner was a wealthy Texan who loved to hunt. He hired me to develop a world-class shooting club on his ranch. In the short span of two years, a bankrupt cattle ranch became one of the premier shooting venues in the country.

Oh, what a view. The guests couldn't lose. Just to spend a day on the ranch was truly a treat, but the hunting was great, too. Gary Ruppel managed the shooting dogs and Ken McGraw did a super job of training and recording the days on Kodachrome.

If we were together there today, I thought, we would be loving the opportunity to share such a tremendous thunderstorm. We would often saddle up after our chores were done and ride into the high country above the ranch.

The old Miller Reservoir was within an hour's ride, and the dilapidated homestead cabin that hunkered against the eastern banks of the lake was a favorite place. The cabin was special, for sure, but if we had at least an even chance of taking in a thunderstorm on our ride, it became spiritual as well.

One afternoon we were caught half a mile from the cabin in an open sagebrush flat. There are many great vantage points to sit out a storm, but out in the middle of a park isn't one of them. That ride is one of my fondest memories. Our horses were as eager to get under cover as we were. What started out to be a brisk canter turned into a dead run through the pasture grass and sagebrush.

The veil of rain was music as it came on a fierce wind to threaten my horse's footing and stifle my breath. My chaps stuck to wet saddle leather. Through my gloves, I read the message of the rein. I remember reminding myself to stay focused, to pay attention. We pulled up in what had once been a corral and yanked our saddles off. We hurried through an open door and laughed amid the scattered ruins.

The storm left as quickly as it came. You see, that's the way it is with thunderstorms, they're always intense, but shortlived. After a few minutes, we were all standing in the drenched grass in front of the cabin to smell the legacy of the rain and witness the calming of the lake.

We swung back onto our horses as the blackness moved to the east. We dropped into the Mesa Creek drainage toward the ranch. A bright sun was doing the best it could to dry us out, but quakie leaves were dripping on us like a leaky faucet as we rode through.

Just before we entered the ranch gate, we saw a big mule deer buck on the hillside opposite us. He knew we were coming, but stood his ground until he saw us emerge from the oak brush. He bounced over a small rise and skirted through thick oaks until he was out of sight.

I decided to see if I could get a closer look at him, and stirred my horse into a lope. We were traveling along a fairly well-used deer trail—I'd be down there shortly. My horse was solid under me, so I started to scan the skyline where the buck had slipped into the brush. We were carrying quite a bit of speed for those conditions, but we were both used to it.

I saw a Y in the trail ahead, and decided to give my horse his head. Whichever way he wanted to go, it was fine with me. He started into the left side of the Y, but for some reason changed his mind in mid-stride.

I had bought the left completely and was already leaning into the turn. This horse was very athletic and agile; his course adjustment took milliseconds. In the space of a heartbeat I found myself grabbing for anything leather. I caught the latigo on the left side of the saddle with my right hand. My left boot was still in the stirrup, so what it boiled down to was this: one second I was looking good, the next I was hanging on the side of my horse while he was running through some of the thickest oak brush in this part of the country.

For the first 50 yards or so, I was praying I could hold on. For the next 50, I was praying I could let go. Somehow I crawled back aboard and considered myself lucky to have all of my clothes and most of my skin still with me.

I laughed to myself as I remembered what a great experience the Buck Point project was. "I never did see that buck again," I told my dogs. They were laying with their heads between their paws, patiently waiting for me to quit worrying about the weather and get the show on the road.

I moved out into the open and the dogs jumped to their feet. "Okay, okay," I said. "Let's give it a whirl, but remember, it was your idea." I tapped them off before giving my gear a once-over. I was making sure I had my slicker.

Both of my dogs were white-and-liver English pointers. The younger of the two had been turning in some stellar bird work in this, his first full grouse season. I had named him Stoney, after the best friend I ever had. He was mostly white with light ticking, and an evenly marked liver mask. The other dog was marked fairly heavily and also was the benefactor of a beautifully even liver mask. His formal name was Elhew William—he was Billy to me.

They threw a wide loop into the wind and broke into separate hunts. We circled above a park called Little Basin, a favorite of late-season birds. Out in front of that storm, the wind was really picking up.

The dogs looked like they had something going. Both of them were doing some major fishing just underneath the cornice of the park. It took me a minute to swing through a patch of quakies and gain enough elevation to see what was going on.

Billy was down hard, twisted into the wind. His head was high, he was drawing deep. I guessed the covey to be a ways in front of his reaching nose. Stoney had the perimeter covered, backing from the cornice. I saw him glance at me as I worked to the dogs with the wind at my back. It was gusting now, flapping my sleeves and pushing me down the hill.

Which is greater,
One or the other.
To believe in yourself,
Or trust in your brother

"What you got there, Billy?" I was talking softly while I looked hard into the cover. One more step...here they came. Five grouse lifted into the wind. They barely got to eye level before they were ripped through the air like shingles in a tornado. Without so much as a single wingbeat, they sailed into the quakies below.

"Man, I hope their brakes are working, Billy," I said to the pointer, his long thigh muscles quivering. I think he was as amazed as I was at how fast those birds left.

Birds breaking on a wind like that are almost bulletproof. Shot patterns can't deal with a force like that. Shot strings might swarm from the barrel with bad intentions, but they are soon disoriented and left to fall harmless. "I couldn't have missed that bird," I've heard shooters claim. The real truth is, they couldn't have hit it.

I started to my left...that was all the remaining three birds could stand. They jumped into the air and peeled off like fighter jets.

"Wow, that was some covey, guys, exciting stuff." I gave a couple of short "teets" on the whistle as I touched Billy on the head. The dogs sprang from their positions and screamed to the front.

That was all of the easy work. Things were starting to get nasty. By now I knew the storm hadn't opted for staying south of the river in favor of making things miserable for us. It was too late. Even though we were looking into the teeth of Thor, we were committed to Willow Peak.

I wanted to at least take a look at a pretty sloping park that cupped around the west face of the Peak. The trouble with that plan was, the storm and I were racing for the same turf. Stoney came running by me as if to openly wonder if he and I had the same game plan.

"That thing is going to pound us pretty soon, Stone. Let's retreat into the timber and get out of it if we can." Billy joined in with us, and we fairly dove over the ridge into the dense fir timber of the northern slope.

I knew where there was an old hunting cabin that laid off the side of Willow Peak. It hadn't been used in a long time—the owners had built a new one closer to the rim of Frenchman Creek. We were going to get wet anyway, and at least we would be out of the wind on the way down to the cabin.

The cabin wasn't locked. There was no need. I lifted the hasp and pushed the door open. It was hung with old leather straps so it drug on the floor in a half-circle as I applied more pressure and again lifted on the hasp. "We're in, boys," I said. "Let's just hang out here until that bastard blows over."

There was an old metal bed frame along one wall. An ageless set of springs was leaning against the bedstead, and a canvas-covered mattress was rolled up and tied with baling twine.

The woodstove looked to be in pretty decent shape. I tore November's page off a calendar that was long since history, and after rolling it into a tube, I lit one end and held it into the firebox to check for draft. I didn't know, maybe animals had built a nest in the stovepipe or something. I didn't want to smoke myself out of my new diggins.

Within twenty minutes, the old cabin was warming up and I was turning the mattress over and over, trying to decide which side would be the softest. The dogs were sprawled out on the floor, occasionally lifting a head to see what the heck I was up to.

I hung my chaps and my jacket to dry and laid down. I had my hands clasped behind my head as I stared at the log beams of the ceiling and wondered about others who had been there over the years. Directly above my head I noticed the yellow edges of a newspaper sticking out from between the roofing and the beam. I stood up on the bed and pulled it out. It was a *Rocky Mountain News*, in surprisingly good shape. I gently flipped the pages until I got to the sports section. The headline of the day grabbed my attention, and before it was over, I was unable to put it down until I'd read the whole newspaper.

"INDIANS DUMP BRAVES, TAKE SERIES LEAD," read the headline. The date was October 8, 1948. The pitching staff for the Cleveland Indians featured such ho-hum kids as Leroy "Satchel" Paige, Bob Feller, Bob Lemon, and Gene Bearden.

The ace on the mound for the Boston Braves was none other than "Lefty" Warren Spahn. Al Dark was at short.

The Big Eight was the Big Seven then; the football coach at the University of Nebraska was a guy named George "Patsy" Clark.

Harry Truman was still in the White House and Dwight

Eisenhower was still just General Eisenhower. Russia vowed to embark on a world-wide blitz to convert every nation in the world to communism, firewood sold for two dollars a cord, and a big load of coal was advertised for five dollars.

"Wow, look at this, Stone, it says here you can buy a new Ford pickup for $1,900 and a house in Denver for $10,000." He wasn't impressed. "Just think, I could sell you two and pick me up a house and a truck." I was just making conversation while I turned pages. It wasn't all that far-fetched, though. Some things are hard to put a price on.

There was a nice picture of General Eisenhower shaking hands with some politician on the front page. I remembered the story I'd heard of his fishing trip up on the Frying Pan River. It turns out that ol' Ike couldn't see all that well, and he was having trouble seeing dry flies on the surface of the water. His guide tied up a mayfly pattern that had a white parachute hackle that stuck out like a sore thumb. It sort of looks like a Royal Wulff. The general did so well with the new fly that he commented that he would give his house and lot for that fly. Thus the fly was named the House and Lot, or the H&L Variant.

According to the paper, the early morning temperature here in the high country was somewhere around freezing, and it climbed up to 65 in the afternoon. The quakies were in full color, and the big game season was supposed to start the next Saturday.

Sheep and cattle were being moved down out of the high country after a summer on the range, and logging crews were working as hard as they could to get their timber down the mountain before winter set in. Sunrise was at 6:30 a.m. I got to thinking about this mountain, and how things would've looked in October of 1948. The Mormon crickets would've been pretty much gone from the parks, along with the grasshoppers. The rich flora would be dry, and sagebrush and stiff stalks of fescue were probably the only cover left standing.

Blue grouse would have been covied as they moved up the mountain toward the evergreen timber. They would have spent the entire summer out in the parks feeding on the crickets, grasshoppers, wild licorice and elderberries. The cock blue grouse would have spent the summer by themselves, but by now would've joined the migration to the winter feeding ground.

Most of the birds and animals drop to lower elevations during the winter months, but the blue grouse and pine marten keep vigil at the top. I have always wondered why these particular animals were chosen to watch over things until the others moved back up with spring. I know the blue grouse were special, and apparently the Mountain Spirit feels the same. He sends only the most trustworthy to do the solitary duty.

Many writers refer to the grouse as "dumb, but good eating." Could it be that they are mistaking a grouse's trust for stupidity? They see people so rarely, how could they know people are not trustworthy? After all, people don't seem to be much of a predator. Not when you compare them to the predators of the mountain. The humans have thin skins that have to be protected by cloth. They can scarcely walk unless they have leather lining their feet.

The grouse are equipped with grand plumage that is renewed every year. They can walk for hours, across ice and rock, barefoot. Their toes have natural pectinations that spread out like snowshoes to help them walk on snow. Those same feet can hold them high in a tree.

The broad wings of grouse are capable of great acceleration at the flush, yet can sustain a glide that will accommodate the widest canyon. Their camouflage is so good, the grouse can simply crouch in a clump of grass and they are virtually undetectable, even from an eagle's eyesight.

Grouse are not alone to fall prey by trusting people. Today, in any major city, in human domain, one must be very careful not to show himself vulnerable or he will be quickly struck down—and called dumb, for not knowing better.

These birds are as all of nature. They have simple goals each day: find something to eat, find water, and stay alive until dark. Because of the structure of nature, grouse are not near so trusting toward natural predators like coyote, fox, bobcat, and various raptors. When you bring a bird dog into the world of the grouse, the birds appears much smarter, more resilient.

I have watched as bird dogs from across the country were

taken down to size by this "easiest to find" of all game birds. I have seen quail and pheasant hunting champions give in to frustration as they went birdless for days while grouse were literally all around them.

I have seen clay target professionals in their quest for this "easiest to hit" of all game birds. I provided comfort as their egos crumbled down around their ears.

This uneducated bird pulls us to 10,000 feet in the Rockies, and we haven't the decency to thank him. He gives us reason to travel the mountains during the most glorious of all seasons, and we call him stupid. He stands in the road so even the laziest of us can admire him, and we try to kill him with rocks and sticks.

The natural world is very simple, and very complex at the same time. We have always considered ourselves to be better, smarter—but are we really? Life, for all of us, comes down to caring for the family until they are old enough to care for themselves. Showing them how to find food, and good water, and a safe place to sleep. There comes a time for each family to disperse, to go their separate ways. They each need to find a covert that suits them individually, where they can raise a family of their own.

Propagation, from the ocean floor to the highest peak, works the same for all species. So the grouse appears dumb, so what. They live in mountain splendor their entire lives. They eat rich, nutritious foods and drink unpolluted water. They breathe air that city folks can only dream of. They could make it harder on us that seek them out for food, or sport, but thank God they don't. These birds have the ability to enrich our lives and educate us to some of the wondrous qualities of nature that we don't ordinarily notice.

Almost fifty years have passed since the Boston Braves lost the 1948 World Series to a Cleveland team that slumped until 1995. The Braves moved to Milwaukee, then on to Atlanta. They now have vindicated their loss by winning the Series back.

Single players are making more money than both teams combined in 1948. Tom Osborne is coaching the Cornhuskers, and Presidents Truman and Eisenhower are both dead.

Communism has collapsed on itself, and Russia proved no longer strong enough to fight off the world's desire for democracy. In a few short years, Russians have denounced their past and embraced a new wave of independence.

Firewood costs more than $100 per cord, and a new car will set you back twice what the average house did in 1948.

I sat up and turned the mattress. It was dark enough in the cabin to stir me to look outside. I had a long walk in front of me if I was going to get back to camp this evening. I would just as soon stay here overnight and strike out in the morning, but things weren't all that easy. There were other dogs back at camp, and I was sure these two were starting to get hungry. A camp needs tending. You can't just walk away when you feel like it.

I pulled the door open and stood on the porch while I slipped my chaps back on. "Did you guys catch some of that stuff I was reading to you?" I asked. "That newspaper was a real eye-opener, wasn't it?" I was talking back through the open door at the dogs. They were stretching and beating a rhythm on the floor with their tails.

I went back into the cabin to roll up the mattress and make sure the stove was cold. This cabin wasn't much anymore, but it wouldn't be anything if I burned it down.

Let's see now...during the past forty-eight years, men have walked on the moon and traveled to the stars. Complete nations have come apart at the seams, while others were formed by rearranging borders and electing new leaders. Computers now have the job of thinking for us, and our government is in debt by a new word, called "trillion." The ozone layer that protects all life is being destroyed by us...the smart ones.

I was not yet born when the Indians and Braves fought it out in the 1948 Series. I was born in November of the following year. I have no way of knowing when I will die, or what changes will occur in the world until then. There is one fact, however, I'm reasonably certain of: with the coming of October, blue grouse will be working their way toward the top of the mountain, searching only for food, water and a place to sleep.

I made sure things were just like I found them before I drug the door closed and fastened the hasp. The dogs and I started down a logging skid that side-hilled around the mountain toward our camp. The first mile or so was pretty thick timber. I liked the thought of that. When those trees are snuggled up together, the dogs tend to stay close. I'd been doing a lot of thinking in the last little while. It was good to have the dogs near.

Just as we were breaking out into some scattered patches of quakies, the dogs pointed a covey of five grouse. They were all wet and fluffed up, huddled in one track of the road. The dogs were standing side by side next to a great big log, an old survivor of the logging era that had finally given up the ghost and settled for what he could get. The grouse were trying to dry out, so I could easily see them from where the dogs were pointing. I walked over and sat down on the log. The three of us looked at the birds for some time before I slipped my waist cord around both dogs' necks and led them away.

We never did flush that covey. While some things on earth are bound to change, and others can't be stopped, there are still a few that remain...forever.

Once, you looked into the soul
of the Canyon of No Return,
You felt its arms hold you
fast to the rim.
The birds took the promise of life,
and sailed away.
Like the fleeting dreams
of a young man,
They soared, then descended.
They left you longing,
searching for where they had gone.

Yes, once you looked into the soul
of the canyon of no return,
And once, I stood there with you.

The Canyon of No Return

Albert Einstein once said, "Everyone who is seriously involved in the pursuit of science becomes convinced that a spirit is manifest in the laws of the Universe...a spirit vastly superior to that of man...in the face of which we...must feel humble."

I don't really remember what kind of grades I got in science, but judging from my overall foggy recollection, they couldn't have been anything above average. Okay, maybe they weren't even average, but I would've loved to talk to Al Einstein about that. I know this spirit he talks of. I've felt its heartbeat and it has felt mine.

After Theodore Roosevelt's wife, Alice, died in the winter of 1884, he went drifting into the vast unknown of the North Dakota Territory. It was during this time of solace when he discovered what he called, "the masterful overbearing spirit of the West."

This same spirit is what brought me to the cliffs of the Salmon River Canyon today. Teddy worked out the anguish of his heart a little east of here, in the plains of the Missouri River country. It was by the grace of this great natural spirit that he found the inner strength and passion to change the face of the modern world.

This isn't the first time I've traded trail talk with Theodore

Roosevelt. He and I share common memories of the Colorado high country where he hunted bear in 1905. It is my turf now. It is my eyes that squint into the remains of the massive Ute Indian hunting grounds. It's my horse that pulls the sweet fescue into his mouth as we pass by. And it is my heart that sings to the mountain spirit.

From where I stand, I can see the early morning mist above the Wallowa Valley of Oregon. The sun is surely coming to greet the sky above what will always be the homeland of the Nez Perce. One hundred and twenty years ago, they fought until their hearts burst as they were being pursued and annihilated by lessers whose only advantage was unlimited reinforcements and sheer ignorance of natural law.

Today, the story is here to read, the lessons are obvious along the tapestry of the eroded, overgrazed canyonland. Just another bitter lesson, learned a little too late. Once again, the conquerors of an entire nation are left to ponder their lack of foresight, as the embers of their victory fires grow cold.

They say this cliff I'm standing on may be nearly 40 million years old. I don't know...this one looks younger to me, maybe 25 or 30. It takes thousands of years to make an inch of topsoil along these harsh walls, but this afternoon alone, tons would be taken unwillingly to the valley floor by late-season runoff.

You see, the unbelievably ignorant have governed this land for a mere 120 years, and they've done 150,000 years of damage. While I stood on the west-facing rim of the Salmon River Canyon—some call it "The River of No Return"—I stretched my arms to the heavens. I couldn't help but wonder if the misting raindrops that colored my gloves were the tears of the fathers of the Nez Perce Nation, or of the mountain spirit himself.

The Salmon stretched out before me like a glimmering ribbon that got narrower and narrower until it tucked into the darkness of the canyon walls. The river was so far down there, its peaceful impression belied the awesome magnitude and power of the mighty River of No Return. Its own identity would be lost forever just a few short miles downstream as it crashed into the boundary waters of the Snake. Together they would lean to the north until they picked up the Clearwater boiling out of the wilderness of Idaho's high country. I wondered how they tell each other of their own personal journeys, these three great powers. I wondered if they were silently anxious about their future as they lay in side by side and slipped into the Columbia Basin.

They carried their story seaward, until at last they laid their riches along the floor of the Pacific like a caring mother puts her children to rest. They surely must have grieved over the fate of the salmon and steelhead trout that were spawned and raised in the uppermost tributaries of their systems. I wondered if the fish felt betrayed by their own as they were ground up by the million in hydroelectric turbines.

Just a century ago, the salmon who dutifully searched out their home waters each year were beyond number. They were able to play their part in perfection. Last year, one hundred thirty-five made the trip.

Red Fish Lake, located high in the Sawtooth Range, was named after the brilliant salmon who stacked up in the outlet like aspen leaves on the forest floor, like the clouding mayflies of the summer, like the flighting waterfowl of the fall. Last year, just one made the show. A French philosopher once said, "When the salmon vanish, all of mankind is imperiled."

I was numb with heartache as I desperately tried to appreciate the astounding beauty of all I saw. I didn't come here today to stand and curse. I came to watch, and look, and learn, and remember. I came to enrich my heart and expand my understanding.

Sixteen mule deer were picking their way along the canyon face a thousand feet below me. They saw me standing on the cliff and froze to stare and decide for themselves what I came here for. I guess they felt I couldn't be trusted, as they quickened their gait and sent echoing slides of scree into the darkness beneath them. One of them broke off for some reason and started bouncing downhill. I think the most definitive trait that sets the mule deer apart from the rest of the natural world is that trademark bounce.

Speed, quickness, agility, power, and incredible balance combine to make the very best of the briefest moments when the animal actually touches the ground. The goats, sheep, antelope, and wildcats of the mountains are all legendary for their athleticism, but for me, mule deer are the poets of locomotion, the aristocrats of kinetic balance.

I was not alone at the top of this canyon. The greatest young pointer I've ever seen was standing by my side, lost in his own thoughts as we stared out into the haze. He was dreaming his own dreams as he stood up tall and breathed in the message of the wind. A light breeze was rising out of the depths to fill his mind and to complete his vision. His nose was wet with anticipation, and it twitched as his shoulder muscles quivered. He arched up on tight, round feet like he was cut from the rock we were standing on. The tip of his tail waved, ever so slightly, as I touched him on his back and spoke to him.

"We came here to learn, you and I, as we have for the past few months. It will be our last run together, and my special wish is for you to break out today. I know you can't handle the coveys like you will when you are grown, but let's set out to find every bird on the rim this morning. When your story is told, my friend, you will warm the hearts of all who see you run. You will earn the respect of your peers, and you will never go to the field with anyone greater than yourself. You and I have traveled thousands of miles together, from one end of the Rockies to the other. You sleep on my bed and you eat from my fingers. Today I will set you free on your journey to legend, and tomorrow...I will mourn my loss."

We turned and walked to the bluff, where I tapped him off and watched him fly to the front. I didn't really have to tell him this was our last walk. You never have to tell dogs these things. He probably knew a couple of days ago, and I was sure he had dealt with it in his own personal way.

It didn't have to be this way. We had planned to grow old together. Sometimes the trials of life close around your throat so tightly that every breath is a luxury, every heartbeat, relief. Because he was so special, he was also very valuable. Wealthy people will go to the hip for a dog or a horse that will make them look better. He will help me once again to escape the jaws of accountability. He will do his part, and I will be forever poorer for it.

His name was "Grand River Avery," and as his young legs reached and gathered, he was driven to a stunning forward race. He is only a year old, but he already knew the chukar would be near the rim today. He knows how they like to covey and mingle around the green-up of seeping springs. The soft, moist ground is cushioned by lichen even during the winter months. The draw of succulent greenery and adequate water keep the immediate area around the spring littered with chukar sign as they walked and fed. The dried grass nearby scarcely covered evidence of the covey roosting sites.

Avery already understood much about the nature of the wind. He knew that the swirling eddies of the current are always rising in this canyon country. Oh, it may drift into pockets of rock, or lay suddenly still near benches or ledges, but sooner or later it will accelerate to elevation and spread out over the rounded bluffs. Sometimes the wind is provided with a more definite and direct escape to the top. A sharp drainage usually means a tight mini-canyon of its own, and often the wind will crowd into the confines and surge upward.

The crowns of these drainages are very often shaped like half a bowl. The bowl effect is caused by the long-term disintegration of the mountain's parent structure. What topsoil is left is usually laid in the hollow of the bowl.

Truth is forever on the wind,
But its exact location is
often concealed,
And almost always comes as
a complete surprise.

The various species of grasses, legumes, or forbs that remain faithful to the canyon will be most dense where the topsoil binds their root systems. Without the topsoil, the plants have no hope for the future. Without the grasses, the soil, no matter how diligent the effort, has no chance of clinging to the slope.

Above the bowl, the rounded cusp is covered with short, sparse grass that is always slightly bent. You see, the grass reacts to the wind in the same manner as we do. It is unnatural to stand erect in the face of constant wind. If you bend away from it and take up a lower profile, you will extend your stay. In addition, the wind will rise and pass harmlessly over you as it softens and strengthens your purchase.

This study becomes so important because we came here to find partridge. The seeping springs, the windblown bluffs, and the dense grasses of the bowls hold the secrets of the birds and they beckon to the heart of a bird dog like the sky to a pilot, or the sea to a sailor.

Avery was five hundred yards distant when his cresting spirit was cut with the fine edge of favor. He spun into the wind and threw his head up. He was breathing deep, testing his fortune. I knew the birds were far below him. He was fishing as he crouched and quickened to stay hooked up with them.

It takes a year or two of dedicated practice before a dog learns of the wind's precocious nature. Truth is forever on the wind, but its exact location is often concealed, and almost always comes as a complete surprise.

Sound familiar, my friend?

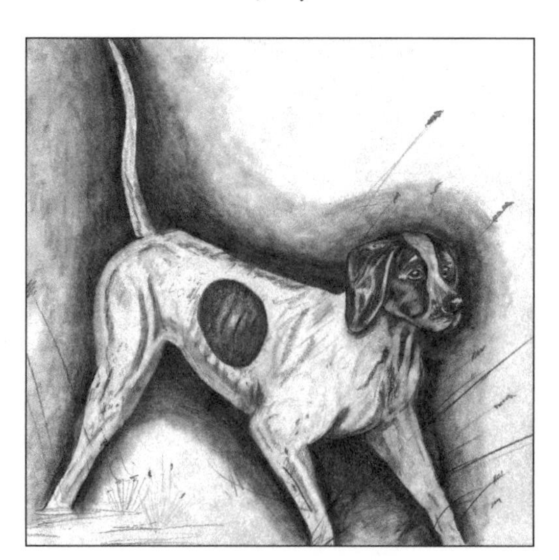

When a pointer is
suddenly stricken,
He not only freezes,
His entire body drops
just a little.

I decided to stay where I was. I had the broad view of things and wanted to watch how he handled his challenge. I scanned out in front of him and tried to predict where success would finally reward effort. He was traversing his ground like an alpine skier. He didn't want to get too far to either side of the magic, but the hill was too steep for a direct route.

He cut underneath a long rock ledge and started working back toward me. I could now make out a small depression between two outcroppings of volcanic rock. I judged the covey to be about two hundred yards from me, and I started moving. It's hard enough to make decent time while you're walking along the side of a cliff, but much more so if you are continually glancing up to check the dog's progress.

Avery circled above one of the outcroppings. I lost sight of him temporarily, but picked him up again as he eased out into the sunlight seventy-five yards above the depression. When a pointer is suddenly stricken, he not only freezes, his entire body drops a little. He stood like he belonged there while I quickly ran through my options. He was still pretty impatient with his birds, and these late-season chukars are plenty jumpy. I could just wait him out and let him learn the lesson at hand, or I could try to get involved and put the covey to wing myself.

I couldn't help it. He was holding his head as high as he could, so I figured that I was closer to the birds now than he was. I spoke to him softly. "Whoa-up. Whoa-up," I cautioned him.

I hopped down off a rock and started for a thick patch of cheat grass that held all the promise of glory. Off to my right, I saw about four chukar on the ground, but before I could take measure of the situation, the air between Avery and me became alive with birds. "God...thirty, maybe forty," I said aloud. Avery charged forward a few yards, then stood, like I was, searching for where they had gone. Chukar often leave you like that. They are much like the fleeting dreams of a young man. They soar, then descend and leave you longing, searching.

"Heck of a covey, Av. Heck of a find," I told him. Avery set about checking the fresh droppings where the covey had been holding until I could get up to him. I called him over to me and sat down on a rock to rest.

"Just look at that, buddy," I said as I pointed to the ridge. "You winded those birds from a thousand feet. You think anyone will believe that? Do you even care? Me, either. Let's get going."

Our emotions swept us upward, like we were on the wind itself, toward the mountaintop. Avery was fairly charging up the slope. The hard muscles of his front quarters were pulling his ground under him in smooth, rhythmic strides while his rear assembly pushed it forever away with driving, powerful strokes. I was smiling as my chest warmed to the pounding of my heart. This walk was going to be all I'd hoped for, and then some.

You have to be careful of your position on the mountain as you pursue grouse or partridge. It is ever so easy to let yourself be drawn to the lower reaches of the canyon by the downward escape routes of these very special birds. They usually break into the wind and then curl down and away until they are swallowed by the depths of relief. Keep your ground, stay to the rim, or you will soon be faced with the unwanted necessity of climbing back to the top.

Avery's eyes were fixed on the skyline until he blasted through the glistening halo of the short grass. I was hurrying to get to where I'd seen him last. I sensed a confidence in his race, and I didn't want to miss any part of it.

As I topped out, I started to frantically scan the mountainside for a glimpse of my young warrior. I was breathing hard and couldn't get comfortable on the thin deer trail that offered meager support to my burning calf muscles.

A coyote started yipping just above me, and he sounded plenty agitated. I quickly gained enough elevation to get a decent view of the scene. I have never really figured out the affinity that coyotes have with pointing dogs. They will frequently yip and howl at pointers, while I've never heard one bark at a retriever. Often coyotes will sit down and watch pointers working distant. Sometimes they will even lay down and admire the dog work as long as things don't get too close.

All dogs seem to alert to coyote sign and some will drop their head and start trailing their wild relatives. That is what Avery was doing, trailing. He was drifting the track like a cougar hound. The coyote was surely hitting out for less crowded hunting grounds, so, for the first time today, I turned my dog away from his effort and gave him new direction toward a wide, grass-covered bowl that bent to the north.

If there were any chukar on earth, they would be holding somewhere within this beautiful bowl that morning. Avery was cutting across the top, just beneath the rim. This cast looked like it would take him over half a mile to where the next dropping ridge was hiding our future from us. I sat down and was quickly taken into a dream as I admired his grace and stamina. I decided to sit there and watch, like a parent watches his son go from one carnival ride to another.

The child is wide-eyed and full of excitement. He is pulling crumpled wads of money from his pockets as he runs to get in line. He jumps into the seat of the ride and grins while the attendant locks the safety bar in place. He waves to his dad as the ride lurches into action, his eyes flicking from side to side.

Avery was becoming a speck of white when he finally decided to loop into the meat of the bowl. He was running with the wind when I saw him shut down. He stopped like someone slammed a door in his face. It was then I could make out several fast-moving gray birds who were making for the cliffs for all they were worth. He must have run right through the covey. After a short time, he regained his balance and broke into a renewed, more cautious race.

Shortly, he was getting all bird-doggy again as he stiff-legged around some yellow star thistle cover and bore into the wind. His popping tail snapped to attention and he slid into a heart-stopping point.

There we were, seven hundred yards apart, both of us blinded with expectation, both of us anxious about the outcome. I sat there and remained silent. This was his day. This was no time to holler or try to take charge. This was a wonderful opportunity to appreciate the blossoming of this great young talent. There would be plenty of time to do his formal breaking later; he would be under the thoughtful guidance of Gary Ruppel. Gary would know how to hone his boundless natural ability.

Five, maybe ten minutes passed before he considered adjusting his game plan. He carefully moved about ten steps forward. He was walking on eggshells, he knew he was pushing his luck. When the covey burst into the air, he looked all around. I knew he was looking for me. He had his excuse all lined out and rehearsed. He didn't get the chance to pull my leg as to the real reason he decided to move up, but he did learn the value of the lesson the birds taught him. He should've stood there, and he knew it. He knew that if you crowd wild birds, they will bail out on you—especially late-season birds.

If you let a young dog make those mistakes for himself, he will develop into a much stauncher pointer. He will learn to stand off from his birds and give them plenty of room. Learning to find the birds is the key here. Learning to handle them takes practice. He didn't need me interfering with his progress. He had to work most of this out on his own. If he couldn't find birds well, all the manners

What a wonderful thing
to rest, and know
There are clouds just above you,
chukar below.

in the world wouldn't turn him into a decent bird dog.

I figured it was about time for me to rejoin the hunt. I stood up and waved to him as he crossed above me. He was clearly looking for me now, and was relieved to see that I was still in there with him.

We stayed with it for several more miles along the rim until we started our loop back. He found eleven coveys altogether. Some of them he handled, some of them he didn't. We got to see some spectacular flushes and never did get to the bottom of his relentless search.

While walking back, I was becoming more and more aware of the heartache that was easing into my attitude. Tomorrow we would say goodbye, maybe forever.

I slipped my waist cord over his head, and we walked together as I talked to him and told him how much I appreciated him. I wondered how he felt. Was he angry, or upset with me, or did he accept the coming change as natural?

We walked out on a long ledge of rocks that broke straight off into the great canyon. I sat down and dangled my feet over the side while Avery laid across my lap.

"Just look at that, Av," I told him. "I hope you never forget me, or this morning." I rubbed the soft skin under his earflap and stared into the distance.

"Avery...today you looked into the soul of the canyon of no return. You felt its arms hold you fast to the rim. A gentle breeze pulled you toward the rim, and the birds took the promise of life and sailed away. I am left bitter at your leaving. I will always embrace your memory. You burned that canyon today, for every covey that it holds dear. You showed me the grace of an antelope and the enduring stamina of an eagle.

"Yes, today you looked into the soul of the canyon of no return. And today, I stood here with you."

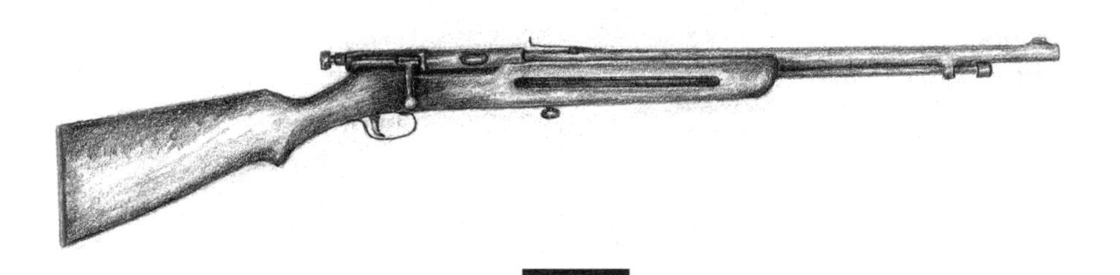

Your first rifle...your first love...
your first child,
For some reason these have always
been one and the same,
At least for me.

Something To Remember

Some things in life are hard to explain. Today, after tending to my dogs, I hung my old .22 rifle in the cabin at Upland Mesa Wildlife Park. The walls are already lined with photographs and reminders of dogs and days gone by. There are pictures of pointers and retrievers who have touched our lives in some special way...pictures of friends, and hunts, we remember together.

A dog's collar from my old Grand River Kennel, one of Delmar Smith's check cords, a collar from Ronnie Smith, Jr., a double coupler of Bill Tarrant's, and a collar that belonged to Bob Wehle all hang in the corner together.

I found an odd horn while I guided Tom and Craig Huff on their first sage grouse hunt. We were exploring the vast Roan Plateau of northwestern Colorado—a desolate wilderness that stirred my soul, both then and now. I'm not sure what kind of horn it is. I placed it on top of the fridge. It lays alongside a whitetail shed antler I picked up in the Paisano pasture of the legendary King Ranch in south Texas.

A ptarmigan and a blue grouse are mounted in somewhat lifelike poses. They represent great memories, not great treasure. The ptarmigan came up with the sun as I stood at 13,500 feet above Ivanhoe Lake. I remember a goshawk was frozen in time directly in front of me as he balanced on a gentle updraft. He glanced my way and glared at me before moving on. With a simple bank and a long glide, his shadow fell across another peak. "It would take me a couple of days to get over there," I remember saying to myself.

I can still see the look on his face. He cast a disgusted stare, similar to what we do to him down below. He didn't leave because he was intimidated—he preferred the company somewhere else.

The dogs and I saw 56 ptarmigan that morning.

The blue grouse is my youngest son's first. He went his first three seasons without missing a blue grouse, an amazing feat for an experienced wing shooter, and much more so for a ten-year-old boy.

This bird reminds me of a special family legacy. Within the heart of the blue grouse lies the legend of the Mountain Spirit, for those who seek it. I close my eyes and visualize bird dogs stretching out across the open parks of the Colorado high country.

Across one wall, an old mountain lion hide tells his story of twenty years of puppies chewing on his ears and tail. He also might recall the day I shot the biggest mule deer buck of my life, for he was there with me. I carry his dewclaw on my whistle lanyard to this day.

Custom fly rods are balanced across a wooden carving of a kingfisher, a gift from Jim Pettijohn. Jim won the world woodcarving championship.

Bill Tarrant's yucca walking stick leans into a corner while decoy carvings and dog statues peer out smoky windows towards Mount Sopris, the 12,900-foot leader of the Elk Mountain Range.

The cabin has no heat, with the exception of a funny-looking woodstove. I try to start a fire in it every day, if I can. Just the smell of woodsmoke brings back so much. Actually, the shape of the stove makes it special. It's very similar to the one my dad used to keep in his main hunting camp tent.

That stove meant so many stories on bitter cold nights. It was that creakin' sound of hooves on truly cold snow, the horses' steaming breath, and air so cold it hurt to breathe. It was great bucks hanging in the quakies, it was the smell of my gloves drying out. It was our alarm clock and our last goodnight. It sustained our spirit, it kept our rifles ready.

It was there that I learned about perseverance. The feeling of wanting to quit was new to me, and it seemed so powerful. Looking into that stove at the end of a day, and being grateful for sticking it out, was important to me then, and it's important to me now. All of the sudden, I remember the last elk we shot together. Now I feel a need to build a fire in that stove.

We had quite a few guns around the house when I was growing up. Some were for this, and some were for that. We used them all. Our guns were more like tools to us. My dad was a trader; he was constantly trading guns for everything he thought we needed. My mom has a Ute Indian bowl made of lava that Dad traded a rifle for.

One time this old .22 rifle showed up in the gun rack. It was in pretty rough shape. I never knew who he got it from. Everyone in the family already had a .22 they liked best. This gun wasn't particularly good-looking, so every time we all went hunting, I sort of got stuck with it. After a time, I hoped they all considered it mine.

I learned to wedge a little piece of plastic under the rear sight and it would shoot perfectly. For over 30 years I used that gun while hunting grouse, squirrel, rabbit and turkey. I shot one bear with it, and at least two bucks in the truck's headlights.

The cabin was starting to warm up as I thought about today. It was 26 below zero this morning. Hard clumps of ice pushed and shoved each other down the river as they passed huddled geese in the frosty mist. There were 87 elk bedded down in the upper fields, along with about half that many deer. While doing chores, I boosted a couple dozen pheasant into the riverbottom, and before the morning was over, I saw 45 rabbits and hundreds of flighting waterfowl.

Yes, today I hung my old .22 rifle in the cabin to remind me of all those fine memories, but also as a tribute to the bounty of today. It is so important to delight in the smallest moments of our lives, because... today it is a moment, tomorrow a memory.

Nice sign...but not specific enough!

The Poacher

My name is Mike, and I'm a poacher.

There is a heavy sigh, and some sobbing is heard from six or seven guys, all sitting in a circle around a campfire. This meeting is an official group therapy session of "Poachers Anonymous."

Oh, don't get all high-and-mighty on me. Every person I've ever met was a poacher of one type or another. These days a guy can get by with his vice by blaming it on his upbringing or some kind of dramatic trauma that happened when he was young.

Maybe his dad made him do chores out in the cold, or maybe he didn't get everything he wanted for Christmas. There are plenty of excuses for slipping into the attitude of poaching, and most of them are fairly valid.

Most people think the poaching habit is reserved for poor folks, those who can't afford store-bought food. It's easy to look down on a poacher as someone who has little or no respect for the law, the anti-establishment contingent. This argument doesn't hold much water, and I can prove it.

Heck, I remember one time a fishing party stomped off of our place when they weren't allowed to keep a trout they caught in a specific catch-and-release area. It was a dandy rainbow—never mind the fact they were trespassing on my neighbor's property when they caught it. Never mind the guide's diligence in explaining the catch-and-release policy prior to the outing. Never mind the gold-medal status of the river.

The person who caught that fish wasn't a chronic lawbreaker, at least you wouldn't think so when you take into consideration that he sat on the bench of the United States Supreme Court.

Far be it from me to bring up the time I witnessed a district court judge baiting someone else's chickens onto his property while staggering around in a drunken stupor.

In fact, I've known of several town marshals and local lawmen who were escorted out of office following the public revelation of their respective poaching tendencies.

Every decent game warden I've ever known was a closet poacher. I've caught them in the act. I've even stood side by side with the game warden while fishing late at night in a private lake. As long as you make sure not to catch a fish bigger than his, you're probably in pretty good shape, as far as the letter of the law is concerned.

How about conservationists, or outdoor writers? I don't care how pure their monthly column is, if you spend enough time with them, they will loosen up enough to let you in on the skeletons in their closet. They all have stories of too much whiskey and too many ducks. Don't believe me? Just cut one of those "ultra squeaky clean, holier than thou's" loose in a field full of pheasant with a good dog and watch from a distance.

I've met plenty of folks who came from all parts of the country in hopes of putting the touch on a trophy mule deer buck. Oh, they bought their license, alright...and they checked the regulations, alright...and they're in the proper area, alright. But just let that buck of a lifetime walk out in the park on the evening before season starts and everybody starts shaking like a recovering alcoholic. They are desperately trying to shake the impulse they thought they had buried years ago while they look around and weigh the integrity of the witnesses.

You say you've never been triggered by such a disgusting temptation. You say you've been hunting and fishing all your life and never broken a game law. Go ahead, keep lying like that and you're going to end up with one of those high-paying government jobs.

Poaching is not always an open-and-shut case, either. It's not always the difference between black and white. What about "incidental poaching?" What about "accidental poaching?" What about poaching out of frustration, or worse yet, defiance? I've seen several cases of poaching out of sheer ignorance.

Okay, I'll let you decide. Take this situation. In the late fifties there weren't many upland game birds around our hometown. My dad, my brother Bob and I were driving around one afternoon looking for some birds to get our pup on. We were starting a German shorthair, and even back then we instinctively knew the secret had to be real contact on real birds.

We saw about 25 or 30 wild turkeys feeding in Clifford Cerise's hay field. Now, Colorado didn't have enough turkeys to warrant a hunting season at that time, but what the heck, we weren't hunting, we just wanted to let our dog see some birds.

We walked the pup over toward the turkeys, and, sensing our pressure, they moved down out of the field into some thick sagebrush. The dog was sniffing and snuffing around, but didn't seem too interested. My dad told my brother to throw a rock down into the sage to get some of them into the air. Bob picked up a rock about the size of a softball and threw it as far as he could. He didn't see the turkeys—he only guessed where they were. The rock hit one of the turkeys square in the back. Come on, now, you're not going to count that as poaching, are you? I would characterize it as "incidental poaching." What do you think?

How about the time one of my training clients came up to the house to check in after hunting the river all morning. He had two of my neighbor's domestic geese piled in the back of his jeep and was very excited about his success in stalking the geese while they lounged on the edge of the river. Well, of course he shot them while they were sitting, or maybe swimming. Those geese couldn't fly if their lives depended on it.

Don't be so quick to judge. He was from Spain and it was his first year in the States. He had a goose license, and, after all, those were geese. I congratulated him on his good fortune and kept my mouth shut as I watched my neighbor search high and low for his geese for the next two weeks. I would have to list this as "poaching out of ignorance."

I've been in the pheasant field with folks who, after seeing their dog point six hens in a row, decided to shoot the next bird that got up no matter what sex, or what species, for that matter. This is "poaching out of defiance."

I knew a grouchy old Italian rancher who had a lake on his property and wouldn't even let his own kids fish there. He was always down at the pool hall bragging about the monster fish he was raising and rubbing our noses in it every time we saw him.

One of my friends, whose dad owned the adjacent property, figured out how we could catch those fish without trespassing. It turns out the ditch that fed the lake was very deep, and it came across my friend's property before entering the Italian's.

We found out that we could pull all the boards out of the headgate and lower the water level on the lake some three feet within a few minutes. We would yank all the boards out and then stand in the ditch with a large landing net between our legs. When the water started flowing back toward us, a number of those lunkers would come with it. It was not unusual to net a half dozen ten-pounders before we finally got nervous and slammed the boards back in place. Pretty clean, don't you think? Good poaching technique, but poaching nonetheless. Besides, some landowners deserve to have their stock poached. I think this was an example of "poaching out of frustration."

Twice I've seen wealthy "sportsmen" ground-sluice coveys of quail to keep from losing a healthy wager with their hunting partners. Both times I was sworn to secrecy—you know, dollars for discretion.

I know a man who dumped two trophy bull elk, even though he had only one tag, just because the elk happened to be standing across the fence from his legal hunting area. Again, the right lawyer and the correct number of zero's on the check kept the thing from seeing the inside of a courtroom. Both of these incidents could be called "poaching by affluence."

I know you might find it hard to believe, but your mild-mannered neighbor just could have been up all night seining bass out of the pond on the municipal golf course.

How about this one—let's say you're hunting quail, or maybe

partridge. You're having one of those good days, you're one bird short of a limit and you've only been out a couple of hours. You feel so good about yourself, you start getting cocky. You may even start holding it over your hunting partner's head. All of the sudden, a big covey jumps right out from under you, and you swing out in front of a decent cock bird to fulfill your destiny. Just one tiny touch of the trigger and it's raining birds. Oops... nice going, three birds in one shot! I don't care how far out in the sticks you might be hunting, I promise you will look around for several minutes before picking up the overage. If some variation of this scenario hasn't happened to you or one of your friends, you haven't been bird hunting much. So this was poaching, you say? Oh, come on, call it what you want, that was a hell of a shot.

When I was young, I didn't really consider shooting deer out of season poaching. At that time, deer were everywhere you looked. Most of the families in our part of the country shot deer regularly to keep a stock of meat. I can still remember how shocked I was when I found out people ate beef. "Why would you eat your cattle?" I remember thinking. You milk cows...you eat deer. Anyway, it just didn't make sense to me.

Okay, so it's technically called poaching. This so-called poaching provided great family entertainment. Poachings were always fine events. All of us kids wanted to go along. We always favored a certain route through the ranchland. It was like going on a Sunday drive, only late at night.

There was lots of laughing and fun talk of memories while we followed the sealed beam across the fields. My dad liked those old Hudson cars because every one we ever had was thoughtfully outfitted with a spotlight on the driver's side. It looked like the ones you see on a highway patrolman's car. The controls were near the armrest, so it was an easy thing to operate while driving.

Once we saw a buck we liked, the shooting was always left to the most experienced shooter. There was never any fighting of bickering about it; we just accepted it as law. We were along to spectate and enjoy the fun, but we were also there to work.

Dad didn't believe in flashlights, so we generally would look for the downed deer with kitchen matches. Do you know how hard it is to find a deer in the dark, using only a kitchen match for light? You had to be pretty darned good at marking the buck down before you jumped the fence and started out into the field. A kitchen match only burns for a minute or two, so you had to be pretty close before striking it.

We carried a gun out there, you know, to finish him off if we had to, but it was frowned upon mightily if we had to use another shot. One shot is hard to hear in the middle of the night, but two or more will surely wake up the rancher.

It's worth noting that there are a few elements of danger involved in poaching deer. You might suffer the local embarrassment of getting caught, or you might break a leg dragging a buck across an irrigation ditch, or worse yet, the buck might not be dead. If he's not, chances are he's got a real problem with you field-dressing him.

While a couple of us were out taking care of the buck, the driver would take a leisurely drive along the country road until the instinctive timer in his gut told him to cruise back to the scene of the crime. He knew just how long it would take to find the buck, get him dressed and drug to the road.

The person doing the field dressing had a very important job. He was expected to do a first-class job of dressing in the dark of night, without losing his knife, and with the help of maybe one more kitchen match.

Some hunters are proud to get blood on themselves while going through this process. I hear some even wipe the blood on first-time hunters if they're successful. We always felt the need to be as clean as possible. The ultimate job left just a tiny bit of blood on your hands so it could easily be concealed by simply slipping your gloves on.

You can read about proper field-dressing technique. Some say to rest a while before starting. Get comfortable. Some recommend a portable block and tackle, mesh sacks, and other such accoutrements. Yeah, right. My brother Art could dress a deer, slip his gloves back on, and be heading down the trail with him in less than five minutes, with or without your help.

Bucks are a lot easier to drag than does, because the antlers make great handles. Besides that, we never even considered shooting does. It was sort of taboo. I guess even poachers have some pride.

If everything works right, you make a mad dash for the road and just as you throw the deer over the fence, your ride shows up. In one fell swoop the deer is loaded and everybody's aboard before the rig stops moving.

Sometimes when we were going night fishing or deer poaching, Mom would make a picnic lunch, and all the family would go along. It was a nice family outing. I remember visiting relatives on Sunday, and after having a nice dinner, my mom would visit with my aunts while the menfolk would go look for a buck. I thought it was interesting to see how my uncles did their poaching.

And by the way, I get pretty sick and tired of people talking about how tacky and unsportsmanlike road hunting is. Proper poaching requires a lot of skill—secrets that can only be learned with lots of practice. For instance, poaching speed is hard to describe. You must drive fairly slowly, so you can check out all the cover without drawing attention to yourself. I figure twelve miles an hour is about right. An aspiring poacher must learn to drive at poaching speed without looking at the road or the speedometer. He must learn to feel for the soft edge of the road and make adjustments without looking up. Poaching teaches youngsters not to slam doors or talk loudly. Poaching teaches discipline. A kid has to keep his mouth shut, even at school.

Many winter afternoons we drove at poaching speed along snowpacked country roads. We were hunting rabbits while we checked out the spectacular mountain scenery. I ask you, what's the matter with driving desolate country roads in Nebraska looking for that dark head of a rooster in a weed patch?

Man has always been a hunter. Prohibiting hunting or guns won't change that. If you take away his gun, he will resort to knives and spears. If you take those away, he'll be back to clubs and sharp sticks.

History teaches us that as soon as a king gets crowned, he starts hunting another smaller country to conquer. As soon as a new president is elected, the other party starts stalking his position. They look for his habits and his weaknesses. They search for his achilles heel, the one thing that can bring him down. If they find nothing, they make something up. It's like bait, to draw him out of cover.

Yes, it's true that some hunters are wasteful and ignorant, but it's not because they are hunters. It's because they are people. I don't care what magazines or books you read, and I don't care if you dream of being the consummate purist sportsman. I hate to break this to you, but you don't just come out of the ultimate outdoor outfitter a full-fledged sportsman. Even though you may have purchased several thousand dollars' worth of the best gear known to man, there is an abyss between you and the man in your dream.

You can't go from a starting point where you are just learning about the arts of hunting and fishing, to a wise old naturalist who softly draws on his pipe without going through a stage where you want to kill everything in sight.

If you see a huge trout in an irrigation ditch and you have this uncontrollable urge to beat it to death and have it mounted, don't worry about it. That's considered normal behavior. The fish cannot become sacred to you without first being abused by you.

Let me put this another way. Cruising Main Street waiting for the local girls to show for the evening is not entirely unlike cruising backroads in an old Hudson, occasionally splashing a spotlight across your neighbor's hay field. I think it's a bona fide tossup as to which is more dangerous or immoral.

Poachers, take stock and save your reputation. As for those who think of poachers as killers and substandard human beings...don't be surprised if you see an old Hudson easing through your neighborhood in the middle of the night.

Let's say he's driving slow at, oh, about twelve miles an hour. Maybe it's someone looking for an address. He might be lost and needs directions. But then again, he might be a poacher, and you might have something he wants...heh heh heh heh heh.

Sally and the Colonel

I guess, the way I see it, The beauty of a bird dog goes a mite further Than skin deep.

We all meet a lot of people as we go through our lives. Some we scarcely notice, some may hold our attention for a time, and a few will influence the way we think and act for the rest of our lives. I will tell you of one of the most distinctive men I've ever known and how we came together in August of 1988.

I was inspired with the coming of fall that year. I was starting to pull out of a two-year nosedive. My dog training business was hectic, to say the least, and the grouse were having a good year in the high country.

I needed a good run. I had been banged up pretty bad while trying to do business with some rich folks and needed to heal up some. Under the auspices of doing good business, that crowd routinely lays waste to honest, hardworking people without missing a bite of lunch.

My wife Holly and I broke away from the bondage in 1986 and set out to develop our own wildlife enhancement project. We decided to turn away from conventional financing and do business on cash flow alone. We believed in going out there every day and making a stab at success by doing as good a job as we could, seven days a week.

We called our project "Upland Mesa Wildlife Park." We started on a couple thousand acres down in the Colorado River Valley, but by early 1988 we had moved the operation up to Carbondale, Colorado.

The ranch we were setting up on was very familiar to me. I was born just ten miles downstream and went to school in Carbondale until they finally got enough and gave me a diploma.

I had actually lived on the ranch during the summer of my first year in college.

The ranch was now owned by a big corporation. This company came into western Colorado with the intention of exploiting the vast oil shale resources while they spent as little of their money and as much of the taxpayers' money as was possible. They had a reputation for burying plenty of little folks as they moved into the valley. Their backtrail looked somewhat like the devastation after 2,000 buffalo have stampeded through the prairie grass.

The federal government was nice enough to extend a real estate opportunity to about twenty oil companies. They could buy all they wanted of the northwestern corner of Colorado for the tidy sum of $2.50 an acre. Heck, oil companies are rich, so before long hundreds of thousands of acres were theirs and the public was left scratching their heads over a deal that, for some reason, didn't seem quite right.

With full subsidy from the feds, the oil companies started exploring the entire northwestern corner of the state. Right off the bat, they discovered there wasn't a whole lot of water in that country, so they decided to buy up senior water rights on upriver. You see, that way they could run their processing plants downvalley and who cared if it dried up all the ranches in the high country.

The ranch that would act as the headquarters of my project was one that had been bought for its deeded water rights alone. Without the benefit of decent foresight, I signed a ten-year lease on the Carbondale ranch and about 60,000 acres of a region known as the Roan Plateau.

The ranch had been pounded by cattle for at least fifty years, and it was in very rough shape. Sure, the fences were falling down, and the road was impassible when wet. Sure the outbuildings were dilapidated and pretty much unusable. Sure, noxious weeds were taking over the hay fields, but somehow I saw potential for greatness.

The house was a complete wreck. The first day I was there, I had to run a cow off the back porch. Cows were laying all over what used to be the yard, and they had either eaten or destroyed any vegetation that dared to break through the dry, packed dirt. Cows are a lot like monkeys in that respect—what they can't eat, tear up, or wallow, they urinate on.

The house had a coal-fired furnace that couldn't be left unattended for ten hours without a complete and major overhaul. Even when it worked, it belched black smoke into the living room and the only bedroom that was furnished with a heat vent.

When I inspected the spring house, I found dead animals, sticks and weeds clogging the water intake. The pipes had been frozen and fixed so many times that the tenants gave up and were draining the kitchen sink into a five-gallon bucket.

The lights and electrical boxes worked, for the most part, as long as you didn't turn on the main light in the living room. If you turned it on, the plastic switch cover would melt within a few seconds.

None of the exterior doors would close, and wind whistled through broken or poorly sealed windows. The lessors promised to reimburse us for fixing it up, and even included the token promise in our lease agreement. That lease looked like hand-crocheted lace when you held it up to the light.

In spite of all the warnings to the contrary, we started cleaning out old chicken coops and hog pens so we could build a new kennel.

We couldn't move into the house right away, so we decided that I would move into an old cabin next to the house until I could get it livable for Holly and the kids. The cabin was dry and all I had to do was spiff up the old woodstove and I was in business. I moved in with 17 dogs.

Okay, taking all this into consideration, why in the hell would I want to mess with this place? Well, because I was a local kid, I knew some things about the ranch that the owners didn't. I knew that the ranch sidled along about a mile of the Roaring Fork River, a famous trout fishery. At the upper end of the ranch, the Crystal River came in and the ranch property slipped along the Crystal for about half a mile of the prettiest riparian area you ever saw. I knew the ranch was the benefactor of at least seven natural springs that fed a series of shallow ponds.

Even though the ponds were bound with algae and cow manure, they were diamonds in the rough. They were ugly and inefficient, but held some of the biggest brown trout in the country. Every guy in town had snuck down there at least once after dark and those fish were hanging on walls all over the West.

I had another ace up my sleeve that could pay off in the end: I knew many of the old ranchers in that area. I knew who built the fence and who irrigated. You see, if you really want to know about a ranch, don't talk to a hired-gun biologist, talk to the guy who fenced it. If you want to learn everything about the water on the outfit, don't go to the water commissioner; talk to the guy who irrigated it. If his job depended on how much hay he put up, he learned how to get it wet, ALL of it. I not only knew these folks, I knew where to find them.

Carbondale's Main Street was only four blocks long at that time, and the old Carbondale Hotel was located dead center. Almost every small town has a hotel on Main Street, and they all look pretty similar. There is always a bar downstairs, and café's come and go every now and then. The stains get deeper in the floor, the bar gets slicker and full of character through the years, but the building is the same and the hotel is upstairs.

The entrance to the Carbondale Hotel was a double door at

the street level. One small step at the stoop and you're in. There were twelve steps to the first landing, then thirteen more to the top. I always wondered why they built it that way, but I counted those steps so many times there was no doubt of the accuracy.

How did I know so much about the hotel? Easy, I lived there for a few years. Forty bucks a month got you everything but a bathroom. I shared a bathtub with five old men who came from everywhere to end up there.

Roy Hungerford was the oldest. I'm not even going to guess how old he was. Jim Darien was the youngest. Roy told how he and others built log cabins, stores and freight stations in the legendary mountain town of Marble, just 30 miles up the canyon. They hauled thousands of tons of marble out of the quarry during the early years of the 20th century, and some of it was carved for all to see at the Lincoln Memorial and the Tomb of the Unknown Soldier. Most of Marble was destroyed by a huge mudslide in the 1940's, and now only a vestige remains of what was once a city of 5,000 or so.

Jim's family sold some land to a ski area developer and cashed in on the big bucks. I don't think Jim ever got his share. He didn't seem to mind much. He always had a smile and a good word for me. I suspect Jim was a ladies' man when he was younger. He never mentioned women, but he was handsome and had an infectious grin. Jim was an expert irrigator. More than once he consulted me, and I learned to value his opinion when it came to water.

Clement Cerise was in his late seventies, and the hotel stairs were hard on him. When he and I hit the door at the same time, I always offered an arm and up we went. Clement weighed in at about 125 pounds, so I could fairly sweep him up the stairs, but I always let him step on every one. It was important to him.

Clement taught me to play "deuces loose" and how to hold my own in pinochle and poker. Those guys liked me, but they would take my money just the same. If you're in the game, you're fair game. Clement would sit behind me while I played cards. If he saw me about to commit to a mistake, he would hock something disgusting from his throat, mix it with a little Beechnut juice, and fire a shot at a spittoon which was always a few inches out of range. I appreciated Clem's advice, but after getting hit in the leg with a couple of those loads, I made sure the target was in reach for him before I settled into my chair.

My Grampa Fuller had lived in the room across the hall from mine. He no longer stayed there, but all of the regulars talked fondly of him. He owned the local pool hall across the side street from the hotel. As a kid I had cleaned spittoons, swept floors, and brushed card and snooker tables for a dollar a day.

The pool hall had a delightful stench that was both penetrating and unforgettable. Darkly stained slat flooring was complemented by a thick, fog-like haze that hung around the dimly lit card tables. I was tolerated long enough to acquire decent skills at snooker and eight-ball while I stood on tip-toes to see across the long green felt. Oh, for a day…if only I could turn an old chair around backwards in front of the wood stove in my Grampa's pool hall, sit still, close my eyes and breathe quietly.

Every small town has a designated bum, I guess. It doesn't seem fair, but nevertheless, he's present, in a variety of shapes and sizes. Carbondale's resident lowlife was Joe Lytle, and he was my next-door neighbor. He was child-like and slightly demented. He never learned to read, write, or count money. If you offered him his choice between a hundred-dollar bill and a four-bit piece, he would take the silver. He just didn't trust paper money, or the people who were always poking fun at him.

He stayed alive by cleaning up the bar and doing odd jobs around town. Some people bragged about cheating him and laughed when he would work all day for free drafts.

He was commonly paid two drafts each day for sweeping out the bar. He would start each day with the intention of doing a complete and thorough job, but his mind would quickly turn to the beer and the second half of the barroom floor was often left untouched. The bartender discovered that he could throw a handful of nickels across the floor before Joe came in to work, and he could be guaranteed the floor would shine from start to finish.

All of these old men were cronies, and they all met every day, either at my Grampa's pool hall or on a long bench on Main Street near the hotel's doorway.

There were several regulars that ambled in every morning, but they didn't live in the hotel. They spent their nights at home, somewhere around town, but rain or shine they were on the bench most of every day.

Jack O'Brien was one of my favorites. He was a professional hobo, and he claimed to have ridden every single spur of the Santa Fe Railroad illegally. He was a true man of the road, and I loved him dearly. He taught me to pan gold and gave me cause to dream as he spun tales of railyards and adventure.

One afternoon, a fellow brought a record into the bar that was recorded of the last steam engine run from San Bernardino, California. Jack leaned into the speakers and held one hand high to hush the others in the room. He suddenly said, "Listen, listen...that old engine is going to start up a steep grade right about now. If you listen close, you'll be able to hear the wheels slip and the shuuu, shuuu, shuuu of the engine trying to catch up."

Jack was right, you could just about visualize the steam clouds rolling from beneath the great wheels with each spin. His face was that of a child on Christmas morning. His blue eyes were snapping as he adjusted and re-adjusted his old cap. The engineer laid on his whistle, and Jack screamed, "Blow that old hog head, hit it again!"

Jack's big right hand was on my shoulder and I could feel his weight fall against me. Tears were rolling down those rugged old cheeks. Damn, that was a great day.

Choppy Lambrecht was a big laugher and was the best hunter of the group. Choppy always drank two beers and then disappeared. He told colorful stories about the birth of Carbondale and other local mining towns, as well as Indian villages nearby. I always thought Choppy pulled my leg more than the others.

Jake Taylor was a leather-faced horse trader. He always drove an old pickup with wooden stock racks. I never saw his truck when he didn't have a slick working saddle strapped to the rack. Jake was always at the horse sale on Thursdays and he kept his saddle handy in case there was a deal for the makin'.

Jake looked like an Indian. His face was deeply creased and his complexion was very dark. He was a cowboy of the Old West, with faded and tattered clothes. The fixin's for his roll-your-owns were always stickin' out of his shirt pocket.

Jake taught me to roll cigarettes. I thought this was a great skill to learn, so I practiced until I could roll them perfect. Before I knew it, I was rolling for the whole bunch. I would roll up a whole can of Prince Albert and use most of a pack of Zig-Zag papers while I listened to their stories and worked on my spittin'.

I always liked to see Chuck Farris coming down the road—always the same, always entertaining. Talk about your cowboy, Chuck was it. Him and Jake were cut from the same bolt of cloth.

He had skinny old bowed legs and a Bull Durham tag a-hangin' out of his shirt pocket. Chuck liked to wear a black turtleneck or a black silk scarf, and most of the time he sported a dirty black felt cowboy hat. I figured Chuck to be the worst cigarette roller in the gang, but they seemed to suit him.

Chuck had a couple of brothers, and each had a unique nickname. One was Hack, one was Sunshine, and Chuck was called Noose. They say Hack was a great bronc rider before my time. Sunshine was a true teamster and continued driving his horses to the very end.

By the time I was setting up my project on the Carbondale ranch, Choppy, Jack, Jake, Clement, Joe and Roy were all dead.

One Saturday morning I drove down Main Street and parked across from the hotel doorway. There were a bunch of signs pointing upstairs, and listed in a glass case at the side of the door were all the businesses who were now occupying the rooms of the hotel. I decided to go upstairs for a look.

Twelve to the landing and thirteen to the top. I closed my eyes and counted the stairs. They might have laid new carpet, but the next-to-the-top stair still creaks—not when you step on it, but when you lift your weight up.

There was an architect's office in my room, a picture framing gallery in Jim's, and...to heck with it, I decided, I'm going down to the street.

They had moved our bench across the street and a couple of hundred feet toward the corner, but there it was. I picked up a

Pepsi and a pack of Beechnut and slid onto the bench. I was in heaven. I wanted to sit right there forever, or at least 'til a familiar face showed up.

It wasn't long. Jim Darien was only half a block away, leaning against the brick wall of the liquor store. Same old smile, same old Jim.

I spit between my boots and hollered in his direction, "Hey, Jim, you getting kinda tired of holdin' up that building?"

He laughed and started walking my way. "That stuff will make you sick, kid," he replied, gesturing to the Beechnut.

"You seen Noose, Jim?" I asked.

Jim always looked at the ground when he was thinking. His straw hat bobbed as he moseyed up to me. He looked up and grinned. "Did you look in over at the café? What ya lookin' for Noose for, anyway?"

"I don't know if you've heard or not, Jim, but I've been working out on the old Coryell place," I said. "I thought I'd buy you and Noose some breakfast and pick your brains a little about that ranch."

Jim settled in beside me and gave me a little elbow jab in the ribs. "There's more water than you'll ever know what to do with out there, kid," he answered. "Even you ought to be able to get that ground wet."

"I was kinda hopin' you would come out and help me get those ditches lined out, Jim," I said. "Most of those ditches haven't been cleaned out in years."

"I'll be glad to help," Jim said. "You know that, but I'll have to catch up with you in a few days. I've got to check in with the doctor over in Denver, should be back next week."

"Sounds good to me," I said. "Want a chew?" I opened the foil of my tobacco and held it out in case he was interested.

Jim laughed as he gimped to his feet. "I switched to gum twenty years ago. That stuff'll kill ya."

"Sure good to see you, ol' buddy. I'll look you up in a week or so. I'd sure like to have you on hand when I turn that water on next year." It occurred to me, as I watched Jim walk down the sidewalk, that I had never seen him hurry. He always walked slow and deliberate. Smooth and consistent—that's Jim. I thought to myself, "That's a good trait."

I pulled up to the curb in front of the café and squinted to look inside. I couldn't see Noose right off, but as soon as I stepped through the door and pulled off my sunglasses, I caught a glimpse of a black felt cowboy hat barely visible over the divider of the corner booth. Cigarette smoke curled up over his shoulder—it was Noose, alright. I walked over to the booth and stuck my hand out.

"You waitin' for your girlfriend, Noose?" I said.

He chuckled as he grabbed my hand with both of his. "Well, I'll be damned," he said. "Look what you see when you haven't got a gun. Have a seat, young fella. How long's it been, anyway?"

"It's been way too long, Noose, I've missed all you guys," I replied. "I stopped by the hotel, even spent some time on the bench with Jim before coming down here. He's lookin' pretty good, don't you think?"

I studied Noose for a minute, and right away I was taken into a dream of another time. I could easily picture him rattlin' up to our house in his pickup and my dad jumping up to go out and greet him. Dad always thought a lot of Noose, and I think that had something to do with the way I got along with him. He and Dad would huddle out by the truck, swap horse stories, and sip on some old low-dollar whiskey. Noose's dad rode the cattle pool up on the Mount Sopris range, and some years they would take a couple of my dad's horses up to take the pressure off their stock.

Noose was one of the first to show up at our house when he heard the news of my dad dying. He made sure I always knew where he was just in case I needed something.

Today he looked the same; he always looked the same. He was some older now, and his whisker stubble was gray, but his voice was warm and his manner friendly. He was wearing his trademark hat and a black silk scarf around his neck. The scarf was worn and frizzy around the edges. He had a denim western shirt on with pearl snaps at the pockets and the cuffs. The flap of his right chest pocket was lifted up on one corner and the Bull Durham tag dangled from a little white string. The last time I'd seen him, the same belt was holdin' up his Levi's, and the buckle was worn so thin it was no longer possible to read what it once said. Black riding boots scuffed back and forth under the table as he talked.

"Buy you a cup?" I asked.

"Why not," he said. "I've got nothin' else pressin'. Do you mind if I smoke?"

"Heck, no, Noose." I laughed. "If I minded your smokin', I wouldn't have come in here." He snatched his fixin's from his shirt pocket and I waved to the waitress to set us up.

"You know, these days it's better to ask about whether someone likes cigarette smoke or not," he said as he measured the tobacco into his paper.

"Let me roll one for you," I said. "That thing's going to come apart and set your pants on fire." I couldn't believe how some of his smokes ever stayed together long enough to get the job done.

He laughed again and flicked the head of a kitchen match with the end of his thumbnail. He thoughtfully torched the malformed effort and dropped the match into an ashtray. Noose's cigarettes would usually flame up at first, and sometimes they would blacken half of the paper before they evened out and started burning proper.

Now, I don't know if you've ever tried to light a match with your thumbnail or not, but if you have, you know there's a certain trick to it. If you don't watch out, that little piece of sulfur will end up under your thumbnail just as it takes off and there's nothing you can do to get it out in time. You will sport a little black spot under your nail for some time before it goes away.

Those old guys would all light up the same way. They'd flick the match and cup it into their palm as they tucked their heads just a little. It's like they were trying to protect it from an imaginary wind. They'd shake the match and usually start talking before the whole thing quite got squared away. Sparks would fly everywhere as smoke poured out from the loose ember.

"I know why you're here, kid," Noose spoke up. "Word's out you're trying to breathe some life into that old Coryell ranch. What ya gonna do down there, anyway?"

"Well," I began, "I'm going to develop a wildlife park while I work on my dog training program. I figure you probably know more about that place than anyone, so here I am."

Noose grinned and shook his head. "So you're still training those bird dogs, are ya? Can you make any money at it?"

"I've never worked the bugs out yet, but you know me. I'm too lazy to work and too nervous to steal," I joked.

Noose told me about the ranch as he puffed on his smoke and wore the waitress out running back and forth with the coffee pot. I glanced at his hands. He was holding his cigarette between his fingers, but out of habit, he held it just above the ashtray so the burning fragments would fall harmless.

I'll never forget the dark yellow stains on the insides of his first two fingers, his enlarged knuckles and the deep cracks in his fingernails. Those marks were the permanent remnants of a lifestyle. They were as much a part of Noose as his hat and scarf.

"You're not feeling too good, are you, buddy?" I asked. It was becoming more and more apparent that something was wrong and there was something Noose wasn't telling me.

"Not too good, kid," he said calmly. "That damned chemotherapy makes me sick."

I couldn't say anything for a minute or two, and I didn't know what to say after that. "I guess I didn't know you had cancer, Noose," I said finally.

"A guy has to die of something." He grinned at his own joke, but we both looked at the table. I fidgeted in my seat and found myself fumbling for words as I played with a scratched-up spoon. Suddenly my eyes fixed on his hand again, and then on the cigarette.

"Sonofabitch, they killed my dad, too," I said. I didn't really mean to say it out loud.

"Yeah, it's one of those cases of too soon old and too late smart," Noose offered.

The sign was clear enough, it was time for me to go.

"So, you gonna come out and help me with those fences or not?" I said, more to change the subject than anything else. "You have to do something to work off your coffee bill. The waitress says you've drank up over fifty dollars' worth."

"Yeah," he laughed. "You probably couldn't get a fence stretched halfway decent anyway. Let me know when you need me. I'll be there."

I slid out of the booth and put my hand on his shoulder. "Take care of yourself, and stay out of the bars, old friend," I said.

I picked up my sunglasses and stared at the floor while a pretty young girl tapped on her cash register and cheerfully asked me if everything was all right. "I guess so," I said quietly.

Two days later, Noose was dead.

From March until August first I kicked the cows out of the river bottom, started excavating new ponds, and tore down every fence I could get my hands on. By mid-August I had built a nice working kennel and cleaned up fifty years of old farm implements and barbed wire. Hunting season was coming on, and I had to be ready to hunt birds on this place by September. Holly and the kids had joined in to help muck out the house and try to get it in shape before school started.

I was working at the kennel one morning when I saw a familiar truck winding its way down our lane. It was Kyle Magnall, a dog-training friend of mine. A big white Ford pickup followed a short distance behind Kyle's rig and came to a dusty stop in front of the cabin.

Kyle hopped out and waved to me as he walked over to the other truck and greeted the driver. After a time, the truck door opened and a white-haired man labored to the ground and reached back for his walking stick. It is my custom to try to get a read on a stranger, so I studied him as they walked toward me.

He was a big man, over six feet tall. He wasn't heavy, but was of broad structure and moved with great effort. He was dressed casually in light brown chino type pants and a dark blue sweater. He wore black riding gloves and a wrinkled-up baseball cap. His light hair curled out from under the cap, and a white turtleneck tucked up underneath his chin. He was wearing soft-soled black walking shoes.

His countenance was friendly but very firm. I didn't know why he was there, but he stood straight up and looked directly at me as he came close. I knew in an instant, this was no ordinary dog-training client. I sensed I was about to meet a very powerful and important person, but I had no idea how important he was to become to me and my family.

"Afternoon," I greeted them.

"Howdy, Mike," Kyle said. "I'd like you to meet someone. This is Randy Blatz. Randy, meet Mike Gould."

I shook Randy's hand and then gave Kyle's a shake before I asked them to come on over and have a seat. We pulled up under a big box elder tree in the front yard, and Kyle began.

"Randy is a client of mine. He bought a German shorthaired pointer bitch from me named Sally. He also had one of your Elhew pointers. Do you remember Printer? Randy was a member of the Buck Point Club and, up until today, was their most frequent patron," Kyle explained.

I was intimately familiar with the Buck Point Club because several years prior I had both designed and built the club for a wealthy Texas doctor. Buck Point Ranch was a fairly exclusive club that acted as an extension of recreational opportunity for the affluent upvalley folks of Aspen and Vail.

Sally and the Colonel,
The magic and
the man.
The spirit and
the wisdom,
I came to understand.

Even though I hadn't been involved with the project for a couple of years, I still knew most of the members up at Buck Point. I had never met Randy, so my first question to him was obvious.

"You must have joined the club after I left there, Randy. I have to say, I'm curious as to what brings you down here to my place?"

"That's easy," Randy started. "I left Buck Point today and I'll never return. I don't like the way the place is being run, and when I spoke to the owner about it, he didn't satisfy my concern. I have a very specific daily routine, which includes an early morning horseback ride and usually a bird hunt with Sally.

"The staff at Buck Point is well aware of my horse's dislike for the sprinkler system, and I requested that they never turn it on until I had finished my morning workout. Without concern for me or my horse, the ranch foreman turned on one of the big sprinkler guns just as I was riding past this morning. He was arrogant and passive when I asked him about it, even though his actions could have caused me serious injury. Kyle says you are very good with the dogs and you are planning to run bird hunts here on this ranch."

"Yes, sir," I told him. "I will run my hunts very similar to the ones we did up at Buck Point. I have my kennel up and running now, and we think this will be a great project to develop. I must tell you though, this isn't the top-end facility that Buck Point is. My wife and I are committed to working this place strictly on a cash-flow basis. We aren't going to build any fancy clubhouses or kennels, and we aren't going to borrow any money to get the job done."

"That suits me," he said. "I'll want you to keep Sally here and continue her training while we hunt with her. I like to hunt every day if I can."

"Did you say every day, sir?" I asked.

"That's what I said," he replied.

We briefly discussed my training and hunting prices, then he turned Sally over to me, crawled back into his truck, and drove away.

I turned to Kyle. "Okay, Kyle," I said, "What's the scoop here, buddy? What happened at Buck Point that made him so mad? Why did he leave such a plush outfit to come down here where I can't even afford dog food half the time?"

"Randy is a special person to handle, Mike," he explained. "He's not the easiest guy to take care of, and sometimes he can get flat cranky. He's very demanding, and when he asks for things to be a certain way, that's the way they'd better turn out.

"You know how ornery Carl Murray is up at the ranch. This morning he turned the sprinkler guns on and nearly got Randy hurt. It's as simple as that. When Randy makes his mind up, it's a done deal. He always pays his bill the minute he gets it, and he tips the dog handler twenty bucks every day."

"How about Sally? What's the story on her?"

"She is well bred, but isn't much of a hunter," Kyle said. "She is a slow worker, kind of like watching ice melt, if you know what I mean. She is birdy and understands the work. I don't think you will have any trouble with her, and she's good to manage in the kennel. Randy is very fond of Sally and won't stand for any abuse. Tom Lovett roughed her up on his first hunt with Randy—his first and last hunt with Randy. Tony Humphry usually guides him and probably knows him better than anyone else. Hey, good luck, I've got to get going."

"Yeah, thanks, Kyle, I'll see you later," I said.

I stood and watched Kyle drive away before I took Sally over to the kennel. Tony Humphry was a close friend of mine and I respected his opinion. I knew he would tell me like it was. Tony is a freelance trainer and usually works up in the Aspen area. He and his wife, Pat, run their own dogs on my place, so I knew I could depend on him to give me the straight scoop.

After checking with him, it turned out that Tony did have a good rapport with Randy and he was happy to give me the lowdown.

"He tips every day, and you can set your watch by him," Tony reported. "If he says he's going to be there at 3:00 p.m., then he will be there at 3:00. He won't show up at 2:48 or 3:05. He's a retired Lieutenant Colonel and his given name is Durand, although he likes to be called Randy. He can be a pain in the butt because he comes every day, come hell or high water. He doesn't hunt very long, and he doesn't really like to kill birds. He loves his dog, and wants to spend part of each day watching her work. He likes things just so, and he's not bashful about saying so. I like and respect him very much, and I sincerely hope the feeling is mutual. I guess that's about it."

Well, that's how I met Sally and the Colonel, an individual whom I grew to admire and respect like no other, and a dog who might have been the best pure bird dog I've ever seen.

Randy phoned the next day to set up a hunting time. He asked if two o'clock the next afternoon would be okay with me, and of course I agreed.

I decided it would be a good idea to get Sally out and take her for a relaxing run so we could get to know each other.

Sally was a liver-and-ticked German shorthair. Her head was marked nicely with an even liver mask covering both sides of her head and ears. She had only one major liver spot on her body, about the size of a softball, just at the base of her tail. Her body was heavily ticked throughout. Her tail was docked slightly shorter than I prefer, but all in all she was attractive to look at and she had a nice running style.

I walked through the river bottom while Sally ran and hunted the cover from side to side. She was a happy dog. I experimented with her acquired, or learned, skills, and Kyle was pretty close. She responded well to my commands, even though she had never worked for me before. We spent the better part of an hour together before I decided I'd seen enough.

I didn't see anything that worried me about this dog. No red flags went up, and her attitude stayed positive and upbeat. I slipped my waist cord around her neck, and she walked quietly at my side while we headed for the kennel. I talked to her in an effort to put her mind at ease.

"I don't care what you've done before, Sally, and I don't care who trained or handled you," I said softly. "Things are going to go nice and smooth for you here."

I was running a little behind the next afternoon and Randy caught me off guard when I saw his truck coming down the lane. I dashed over to the kennel and flipped Sally's gate open. I was still pulling myself together when I met Randy at his rig.

"Afternoon, Randy," I greeted him. "I think we're ready to roll here."

"What a day," Randy said. "How could we have anything but a perfect hunt on a day like this?"

He sat down on his tailgate and pulled a nice Parker reproduction double gun out of a leather slip case. He removed the snap caps and placed them in a plastic cottage cheese container where he had a box or so of shotgun shells. Randy always carried two of these containers, one for light loads and one for slightly heavier loads.

"What are we hunting today, Mike?" Randy asked.

"I think we will hunt some pheasant today and maybe a few chukar. It will give us a chance to check Sally out and get to know each other better."

"What do you recommend for loads? I brought some 7½ and 6 shot."

"I think the 7½'s are plenty over a pointing dog. You might consider loading your first barrel with the light load and then following up with the 6 shot," I advised.

"Will I need a bird vest?" Randy asked.

"Nope, I will carry the birds for you," I replied.

We started walking up the road toward the fields we planned to hunt. Randy walked with a measured gait, and I could tell he was being very careful about every step. He said he didn't like thick grass because it was hard for him to pull his feet through without tripping. He said he could get around pretty well as long as we took a few things into consideration. He could step across a ditch, but sometimes needed support on the landing. I learned to always be there, and from the first day forward I tried to give him an arm when he needed it. Randy didn't like needing a hand. I could tell it bothered him, but he was grateful for it being there nonetheless, and always said "Thank you."

Randy was sophisticated and educated. I always appreciated him not rubbing that in my face. He was always cordial and patient with me. We must have been an odd pair, the worldly old colonel and the mountain kid; he who was at home at the opera and he who played guitar and sang about the sunset. Randy taught mathematics and polo at Cornell University, while I barely made it through high school and dropped out of college.

Randy went against his mother's wishes and took flying lessons when he was only sixteen. He earned his pilot's license in 1929. I learned to drive on dirt roads and still prefer them to the superhighways. Randy sips fine wine and rare brandy, while I'm more at home drinking beer around a campfire.

Most days Randy would play classical music on his way to the ranch and I would turn down the local country radio station when I saw him coming so's not to offend him.

"What do you think of Sally, Mike?" Randy asked that first day.

I told Randy what Kyle had said about her not being much of a hunter. I told him that Sally and I had gotten acquainted the day before, and I had a couple of ideas on how we could give her the chance to open up some.

"If it's okay with you, Randy, I'd like to let her hunt without much interference from us so I can get a true read of her natural ability," I suggested.

"That sounds great to me," Randy replied. "I don't like a lot of noise when I'm hunting, anyway. I am coming down here to enjoy the day and my dog, and if we can do that without whistles and hollering, all the better. You might not believe this, but I don't really like to shoot birds," Randy confided. "Does that sound strange to you?"

"Not really," I said. "Tony told me that you weren't all that crazy about killing birds. I love birds as much as I love dogs, so you won't get any argument from me on that." I was already getting a good feeling from this guy.

"Oh, there is one other thing," Randy continued. "I hunt a little different from most other hunters. I will shoot at the first bird pointed, and then I will give the gun to you for the second. We will trade off like that on every other bird."

"Oh, that's okay, Randy," I replied. "I don't usually shoot while I'm guiding. I normally just handle the dog and take care of the birds for you."

"I don't care what you usually do," Randy said firmly. "When you hunt with me, you will take every second bird. I come out here more to watch Sally than to shoot, and the dog work is always more vivid and meaningful if you're not doing the shooting."

That statement stopped me in my tracks. I've guided over 2,800 hunters in the field and have arranged hunts for another 10,000. Finally I'd met a man who knew and understood the secret to the highest quality wing sport. I've always enjoyed this truth as my own personal treasure, but I suddenly found myself sharing it with someone I had just met.

Yes, it's true, watching and studying the dogs is a much greater learning experience than shooting birds. The shooter sees little but the flushing bird, and even if he misses, he will generally watch the bird until it disappears distant.

The dog handler sees the frost and the cover, he feels the wind and the season. He enjoys the panorama of the event instead of single-minded focus on a gamebird. As the birds spring to flush, he doesn't have to consider the necessity of quickness, and his mind might just as easily drift with the smell of rain, or the feel of wheat grass. Many times the shooters are vastly unaware of their surroundings and miss important factors of their successes and failures.

After our first hunt together, we agreed to let Sally determine our hunt and we made small talk as we walked toward his truck. He separated his shells into the different shot sizes and snapped the plastic lids back on the cottage cheese containers. I always wanted to ask him why he carried his shells in those things, but never got around to it. There were many things I would've liked to know about Lieutenant Colonel Durand B. Blatz that I never got around to asking, and he never got around to telling.

Randy came up with a biscuit for Sally and she crunched away while he ran a Tico stick down each barrel before replacing the snap caps and letting the hammers fall on each barrel. As he slid his shotgun into the case that first day, I had no idea of the significance of this ritual that Randy repeated at the end of every single hunt together.

"Is two o'clock okay for you, Mike?" he asked.

"Yes, sir, no problems here."

"Okay, let's plan on two o'clock for the next month or so," he said.

As I watched Randy drive away that first day, I remember saying to myself, "That wasn't too bad, although he must not have liked it all that well. He didn't give me the twenty bucks."

The following day I was ready. I got Sally out of her kennel at about a quarter to, and was standing at the edge of the cabin when I saw Randy's dust winding down the lane. I checked the time. Damn, Tony was right, two o'clock on the button.

"Afternoon, Randy, how's it going today?" I called.

"Good!" he said enthusiastically. "How could I be doing any different on a beautiful day like this?"

I never heard him complain about the weather or the temperature. Cold weather never stopped him, but slick footing was something he couldn't handle. If it snowed a little or was wet enough to be slick, he would cancel.

You'd think on days when the snow was too deep to hunt birds, a guy of Randy's age would sit by the fire with a good book. Randy loved a good book, alright, but during the snowy part of the winter Randy headed up to Snowmass mountain and went skiing. Every morning he would ride his horse, Socks, for an hour or so, and every day he would hunt with Sally if he could. He routinely worked out on a Nordic Track, a stair step machine, a rowing machine, and skied every chance he got during the winter.

On that second day Randy had two shotguns with him. They were a matched pair of Parker reproductions. One was a twenty-gauge and the other a twenty-eight.

We always loved the smaller gun, and after a while it was the only one he brought. We both fell down with it one year, and it cost him about a thousand dollars to get the stock redone.

First he shot, then I shot, then he shot, then I shot, day after day, week after week, month after month, and finally year after year. We didn't hunt birds in the late winter, spring, or summer, but the rest of the year was fair game. All in all Randy and I hunted together about 350 times. Think about that. Think about all the times you've been hunting in your life.

We tried out every excuse for missing birds you could imagine. Common excuses like "the sun was in my eyes" or "my safety was on" didn't stand a chance. If I made an attempt at coming up with a new excuse, it had to be both original and believable. A half-hearted attempt would only bring a roar of laughter from Randy. Sometimes he would turn his back and chuckle as he walked away, saying "That's a new one, isn't it, Mike?"

Truthfully, I enjoyed pulling his leg. He would give me a hard time about missing easy shots, and after a time I felt comfortable enough to give some of it back.

Randy loved the sea. He told me stories of sailing with his family, and recalled with pride how he could sail into a crowded Boston Harbor under full sail. There were even stories of the America's Cup race.

At 26 years of age, Lt. Col. Durand Blatz was the commanding officer of five battalions during World War II. His stories of the war were always sobering, and they seemed to take him away, also. He would sometimes be reminded of those times, and he would go into great detail about the hardships of war.

One of my favorite stories was when he got a royal chewing-out by General Patton, and later, in private, a word of support—off the record, of course.

He snapped my eyes open with his recollection of being forced down in a helicopter during the Vietnam conflict. A cameraman's strap had inadvertently gotten tangled and shut the fuel off. He said he was lucky to have been with a pilot who was talented enough to "dead stick" a powerless helicopter.

He qualified as an expert, both right and left handed, with the service .45 pistol.

"God, nice going, Randy," I told him.

"Nice going, my butt," he said. "It cost me my hearing."

It was sometimes hard to compliment him, because you just never knew what he was going to come back with.

Randy was an equestrian from childhood. He was riding hunter jumpers at a very early age, and still owns a big horse operation on the East Coast. His daughter, Elizabeth, is regarded as a leading trainer of hunter jumpers. His experience with the equine arts came in handy, as he was the commander of the last mule brigade in the U.S. Army, with 140 mules under his charge.

Randy's personal record of accomplishment is both staggering and astonishing. I know he wouldn't want me to go on about it, but I think his life is a truly remarkable study. Just think about this:

Randy learned to hunt quail with a guy named John Leavenworth, the first football coach of the University of Alabama. He was there before the legendary Paul "Bear" Bryant. He loaned his quail gun to his friends to use, and both General Westmoreland and General Tabor cut their quail-hunting teeth on it. He gave the same gun to my wife, Holly. It's standing in the closet of our bedroom tonight.

(You think this job doesn't have its fringe benefits? I've hunted with Randy, General Tabor, Admiral Ball, several Navy fighter pilots, one Royal Air Force pilot, and twice with General Schwarzkopf. I've shot TV shows while riding with Vietnam War vets in helicopters, and have been buzzed by F16 fighter jets while quail hunting.)

The Colonel's life goes on and on, but he would want me to tell more about Sally. He loved her dearly, and the feeling was mutual, for sure.

Both of us were fond of her to start with, but as time went on, we grew to appreciate her amazing talents as a first-class bird dog. I recall with great fondness the many fall afternoons when Randy and I would stand in silent awe of Sally's ability. At times her work would defy universal laws of nature. Like watching ice melt? Hah! Not much of a hunter? Hah!

After a while, Randy quit driving his truck to the ranch and started driving a Subaru car. Sally memorized the sound of his car and could single it out from a great distance. On an average day at the ranch, over twenty vehicles would come down that road for one reason or another. We provided dog boarding and training, fishing, and bird hunting services. From early morning until late afternoon the dust never really settled on our lane.

Sally was always an easy keeper. She was happy and liked other dogs. She would spend her days relaxing and laying in the sunshine. She loved to carry her feed dish into her house and stash it under her bedding. Every now and then I would have to crawl in there and retrieve a pile of dishes. I liked to keep her in a certain kennel where the early morning sun would shine in and get her going. She didn't bark or whine much, and for the most part minded her own business.

She could be lying in the sun with her eyes squinted to the light when she sensed Randy's car. Her head would pop up and her ears would square off. She would remain motionless until she was sure there was no mistake, and then she would leap to her feet and start spinning and squealing with joy.

I would often sit on my feed table and test her. As soon as I saw her go into the "here's Randy" act, I would stand up on the table and look for him. The lane into the ranch was almost exactly one mile long, and sometimes it would be a while before I could see him enter the lane off of the county road. She was sensing him over a mile away on a very busy county road.

I'd grab my waist cord and bird bag and start heading up the road. It didn't make any sense for Randy to come all the way to the house each day, so Sally and I would usually try to meet him near the fields we planned to hunt.

As Sally and I walked, we could see him stop the car and lift up the rear door. He was always ready when we got there, and after a quick biscuit, he would let her jump up and put her feet on his waist. Randy always had a compliment for the day, a biscuit for Sally, and a kind word for me.

To the casual observer, Sally was a middle-of-the-road kind of dog. She was average size, and she merged into her surroundings so well that she didn't command immediate attention. She possessed a couple of traits, however, that are as good as gold to a bird dog. She would go boldly to her game, but she had the stealth of a cougar.

Sally moved smoothly over her ground and was deliberate in her race. She ran a thorough, searching pattern. She didn't mind being handled, but from the very start, we tried to handle her as little as possible. I know there were times when we would go a month or so without adjusting her at all.

Randy made a very astute observation one afternoon. He said, "She doesn't need discipline very often, but when you give it, it sticks." That was so true. When I did have to reinforce a command or discipline her, it was very subtle and she took it to heart. She would simply come back working hard and she would leave the problem behind her.

Sally had an amazing ability to discern whether a bird was hit or not. She would normally not chase after a bird that was missed cleanly, but she would stay with a long sailer, and without fail, bring it back.

I was handling a couple other hunters one day when I saw the manifestation of this trait like I've seen in no other dog, before or since.

One of the hunters shot a rooster pheasant but his pattern was far enough behind to barely wobble him from the wing back. The pheasant kept on and flew across the field we were hunting, then the next one adjacent, across a six-foot irrigation canal, up a thick brushy hill, across the county road, and finally fell stone dead about 150 yards above the road in a juniper/pinyon forest.

Sally had the same view as the rest of us, but somehow she determined the bird was coming down. She dashed across both fields and swam the ditch. She skidded under a barbed-wire fence and fought through the brush to the road. Without a glance in either direction, she charged across the road and disappeared into the trees.

The hill above the road is very steep, and I knew the chances of her driving deep enough to complete the retrieve were about nil. I couldn't believe she had carried the line as far as she had already. The three of us stood there staring into the distance. I was holding my whistle just outside my lips. I don't know why, because she was far out of hearing range.

I've trained over 3,500 dogs for the sporting public, and I've worked just about every breed you can imagine, but I've never seen a marked retrieve that came anywhere close to the one Sally did that day.

After a couple of minutes of suspense, she showed up on the road, heading our way with a dead pheasant in her mouth. That mark was well in excess of half a mile. That retrieve was 100 percent natural ability.

Sally was wonderfully confident on her birds. Occasionally Randy and I would come up to her point and the bird just wasn't there. I would stomp around in the cover while Randy's hands went numb around his shotgun. I would make bigger and bigger circles and end up again looking closely into the cover immediately in front of her nose, but still no bird. I would tap her and tell her to relocate, thinking it must be a running rooster. Sometimes she would quickly relocate, but usually she would refuse to move. If Sally wouldn't move, the bird was there. Those searches seemed interminable, but just when I was ready to call her bluff, a big rooster would cackle into flight. By then Randy was so stiff that the chances of him getting his pattern on the bird weren't good.

Sally was the best trailing dog I've ever seen, bar none. If she got a noseful of a running bird, it was only a matter of time until she got him pointed. I guess there were probably a few birds that outsmarted her, but it happened so infrequently that we never really worried about it.

Sometimes we would spend the better part of an hour watching in silence as she worked her magic. I can only imagine the frustration some of those wise old roosters felt. They would try every trick in their bag, and in the end, they were face to face with a decision that they didn't want to make.

I'll never forget a time when I was brought a five-year-old German wirehaired pointer for training. This dog was owned by an upvalley know-it-all, and he claimed she was a fairly decent working dog who just needed some touching up.

I ran the dog through some routine yard drills, and then took her to the bird fields. She didn't seem to have much of a nose, and even when I could see the birds on the ground, she didn't produce a find. I planted game birds for her, and still she couldn't find them. She was about totally useless as far as a bird dog goes.

I called the owner and told him the story. He puffed up and declared that this dog was proficient in the field and he was certain

I'd done something to ruin her. I asked him to come down the following day to test his dog.

Just before he was to be at the ranch, I set a dozen pheasants in a field of medium cover. I asked him to hunt his dog like he normally would so I could witness for myself my obvious misreading of his dog.

The dog's owner brought one of his friends to accompany him on this hunt. I walked along with them as his dog snuffed and sniffed for almost three-quarters of an hour without so much as getting birdy. They covered every square inch of the field with no sign of a bird.

He was making all kinds of excuses why the dog wasn't finding birds. "They must have left the field...it's getting too hot...she's worried about the pressure...she hasn't been hunting yet this year and hasn't reached her stride."

Finally he started to zero in on me and accused me of not releasing any pheasants just to prove my point. I asked him if he would mind if I brought out another dog to check the field, and he quickly agreed. He was clearly embarrassed and flustered, but little did he know, it wasn't going to get any better.

I hustled over to the kennel and grabbed Sally. I casted her into the same field that had been worked over and over by three people and one dog with no success. She pointed and retrieved thirteen roosters. Remember, I only released twelve!

I never saw the guy again, but a few weeks later, I heard he had bought a new German wirehaired pointer from the same breeder. A man's ego is a spooky thing. I shared the tale with Randy the next time we got together and we both felt the exercise was enjoyable.

One glorious morning Randy and his wife, Jody, joined me in the high country while I was working the dogs on grouse. I worried about this a little, because I knew Randy couldn't handle walking in those mountains. Nonetheless we were there together when daylight stretched out across the parks above the Deep Creek Canyon. I brought some other pointers up there with me, but the first order of business was to try to get Sally into some birds. We weren't hunting, rather we were just enjoying a view I've never really gotten used to.

We were unloading dogs and getting ready to work a gradual sidehill just below a park I call the Gentian Forest. This park usually holds a covey or two of blue grouse, and with any luck, today would be no different. I dropped Sally out of the dog box and went about finding a suitable bracemate for her while Randy and Jody were easing out of their car.

Randy always had a special look on his face when he was reveling in a moment, whether it was following one of my more elaborate excuses for missing an easy shot, or when he was simply very impressed with what was happening. They both were accustomed to great mountain scenery, being how the view from the front deck of their house is both extraordinary and inspiring.

From where we stood, the park was a sparkling wonder. Tall fescue grass and a multitude of wildflowers were dazzling as the early morning sun lit up a light covering of hoar frost.

As Sally dashed into the fescue, the frost was shattered into the air and left to softly settle back to earth. This poor man's jewelry makes for brilliant, ever-changing prisms of light that leave you wishing they could've lasted just a tiny bit longer. I glanced toward Randy. There he stood with that certain look of fulfillment, and I was glad he was there with me.

A dog handler's obligation is that of the dogs, so I spun to locate them, both Sally and a two-year-old pointer male that was down with her. There—a scant twenty yards from the vehicles, they were standing tall, leaning into a soft swirling breeze.

Tanner had the birds and Sally was backing. I wasn't completely sold on the find. It seemed too soon, but there they were, a beautiful hen blue grouse and six of her fourteen-week-old poults. I looked back at Randy. He was beaming. It was then I was sure he was glad to be there also. I think we saw about thirty grouse that morning. I'm sure Randy and Jody were off the mountain in time for a late breakfast together in town.

From day to day, and from time to time, we learned about each other as we learned from each other. We always had this wonderful common bond, this one unmistakable quality of measurement: Sally.

She continually thrilled and surprised us as we studied her maturing abilities as a bird dog.

I'll never forget the time we got to witness, first-hand, her remarkable skill of manipulating the situation to suit herself.

We were hunting chukar one afternoon just after the hay had been taken from the fields. The fields were cut very short, so we were concentrating on the weed-filled banks of the irrigation ditches.

Sally had been making game for quite some time and was actively trailing. We had seen this act from dress rehearsal to final curtain many times before, so Randy was slowly walking down one side of the ditch, and I the other.

I looked far to the front and saw a pair of chukar had popped out of the ditch and were sitting about five yards out in the hay field on the upwind side of the ditch.

This was a feeder ditch, so it was getting narrower and shallower as we went along. The birds were near the end of the ditch, so I'm sure that played some part in their decision to change tactics. They had been fairly comfortable with the running-and-dodging technique for a long while, but now the call was clearly for a change in plans. I'm sure they would be satisfied to let Sally move past them before they jumped back into the ditch and sprinted down the backtrail. The old leave-the-way-you-came trick has been the undoing of many a fine bird dog.

The ditch was only about a foot deep as it passed by the holding birds, so it would be no problem for them to watch her pass before they split. The only real problem the birds had was that Sally was thinking way ahead of them.

Randy and I stood and watched as Sally dropped to her belly and literally crawled past the waiting birds, who were totally unprepared for what was about to happen. The birds were frozen, but they had to feel pretty good about their plan so far...that is, until they glanced over their shoulder and saw Sally crouching into a point directly behind them. They held their ground as they endured the heat from her stare. It was finally too much for them, and they sprang into the air. Randy got 'em both.

"Did you see that?" Randy said.

"I sure did," I laughed. "You're not gonna call that a double, are you? Heck, Sally did everything but load your gun for you." We both laughed.

Although we had ample opportunity, we didn't shoot any more birds that day. We didn't need or want to. We were lucky enough to watch Sally go through that same routine on other occasions, but that first time was special for both of us.

We figure we saw in excess of 3,000 game birds over Sally's points. We saw spectacular trailing and tracking jobs. We saw points in culverts and in trees. We watched her creep through snow and heat both until she would finally button it up just beyond the bird's frantic effort to remain hidden.

Sally was a true master of the scent cone, and could accurately gauge the pressure she was applying to the bird. She instinctively knew when to press and when to let up. She knew when to circle and how far out to circle. I've never seen another dog who could handle birds as confidently from the upwind side of the cover as she did with the wind in her face. It was no compromise to run her on the upwind side of a weedrow. The benefit to the bird was minimal.

Of the thousands of opportunities I've had to watch Sally handle her birds, there were many dramatic and unforgettable events. She was so complete in her own special art form. She stood without peer, all the while humble and helpful. She reminded me of people I'd known who had been branded with unfair commentary of their character, only to overachieve and prove the depth of it.

Though I'm sure Randy has his own favorite memory of Sally's work, I feel bound to tell of my own.

I love dogs and the work they do. I respect their lives and the value God has placed on them. My beloved friend Bill Tarrant says; "The dog has all the attributes that God said men should have, but don't—loyalty, steadfastness, love, dependability, patience, etc."

As a person who has handled many dogs, and many breeds of dogs, I've come to accept some pretty remarkable feats as commonplace. I have heard so many dog stories that I can generally finish for the storyteller when he is only halfway done explaining of his dog's heroics. This is not to say I take the story lightly, and I appreciate their taking the time to tell it to me, but it's just that many of them aren't all that spectacular.

To me, one of Sally's finds ranks above all others, and this is how it happened:

Sally was working a rooster pheasant one afternoon while Randy and I followed along, quietly taking stock of an otherwise uneventful hunt. We had worked along a series of ditches where Sally was obviously having some trouble discerning which direction to take her effort. She hunted up a ditch and then looped far to the rear as if to say she was questioning her read. She disappeared in a deep ditch and was gone for some time.

When Sally would remain out of sight for any length of time, it usually meant she was holding her birds somewhere in a ditch. All we had to do was find her.

Rather than having Randy needlessly walk up and down the ditches, I would strike out to locate Sally, and then I would signal for him to close in for the shot. If it was my shot, Randy would lean against his walking stick and watch from a distance, hoping for a miss.

You must know, Randy developed a theory that was later upgraded to a full-blown law. He always figured that as soon as I committed to a certain direction and went looking for Sally that way, the bird and the dog were most definitely located in the opposite direction. I could often hear him chuckling as I walked, and searched, in cover where any normal bird would be holding, and sure enough I'd end up finding Sally after giving up on my plan and reversing my field.

Well, that day Sally had been gone for a long time. I looked and looked, but couldn't find any trace of bird or dog.

The ranch water system was fed by two major canals. Both of them were at least five feet wide, and during the irrigation season were a couple feet deep. The big canals were full today, but in many places the cover was very dense along them. I decided to check up and down the closest one in case Sally had slipped out of one of the feeders and hunted the main ditch.

I had walked a long way into the wind and was preparing to come all the way back to Randy in an effort to start the whole process again. She had to be there somewhere. I must have missed her. Sally was very heavily ticked, and she sometimes would blend into the cover so well that it was hard to pick her out.

I looked toward Randy. He was a couple of hundred yards from me, patiently waiting. I checked the wind again and again. It was fairly brisk that day and had a crisp bite to it. I knew there was a storm moving in from the west. "I hope I find her before winter sets in and freezes ol' Randy solid," I joked to myself as I retraced my steps and tried to look closer than I had before.

I stopped at a head gate where several feeder ditches merged into the main canal. The smaller ditches were gated off, and were nearly dry. There was a tiny bit of wet mud along the bottom of the feeders and I could see dog and pheasant tracks going both directions.

I was just getting ready to jump across the big ditch when I saw Sally. She was on point. She was standing mid-stream of the big ditch. The water was so deep that it covered her entire body with the exception of the very tip of her tail and her head. The water was moving with such velocity that Sally had all she could do just to hold her ground.

I waved to Randy. "You've got to see this," I hollered.

Sally was glaring into a small clump of tansy and reed canary grass that was hanging onto an overhanging bank directly across from me. I don't know how long she'd been there, but she stood another five minutes as Randy negotiated a couple of smaller ditches and made his way to us. We were moved and astonished at this incredible find, but were equally impressed with the courage and the intelligence of the pheasant.

This immensely talented creature was pitted against maybe the only dog who could get him set. When he finally selected a site more suitable to a muskrat than a game bird, she relentlessly sought him out. She stood in nearly freezing water as it rushed about her, and over her, until I jumped the ditch and put the bird to wing.

By the way, we missed him and we were both glad we did.

Even though I had proved to be an elusive target for the corporate triggermen, they were slowly but surely settling their crosshairs on me. Inevitably they started grinding me up.

I liken the corporate structure to a turtle. The corporate underlings, the wannabe's, will slither out from under the parent shell just long enough to take a piece out of someone and then quickly retreat back to the safety of the shell. There is no identifiable trace of them ever leaving the mother body.

The corporation stands to lose nothing. If one of their cheap-shot artists is caught out by himself, they simply deny his existence and the next day when he shows up for work, no one remembers him.

Upon consulting with my lawyer, I found the company was indeed breaking my lease agreement and I could prove they were doing it intentionally. I had no money, but I wanted to fight.

Although I tried very hard not to bring my personal problems to the field with me, Randy always knew when I was deeply concerned about my situation. He told me not to worry about things I could not change. "Think of your blessings, Mike," he told me. "You're young and healthy, you can work and you have a good reputation. You have a great family who loves you. What else could you ask for?"

"But, Randy," I protested. "I had hoped this time it would be different. This time I was actually making a future for my family. This project is really taking off. These guys are deliberately cutting me off. Don't you think I have to fight?"

"You're crazy if you do," he replied. "You can't win. Besides that, you already have everything that's worth anything. What could you possibly gain?"

For the first time I felt frustration towards Randy. "It's easy for him to say," I told myself. "He's lived a life of substance. He's acquired everything a person could want in life. He is wealthy and well respected. He also has a great family that loves him, and he enjoys a sterling reputation." I wondered if Randy ever knew how it feels to poach deer and pick spuds to feed his family.

Once I shared with him a trip I took to town. I pulled into the parking lot of a Firestone tire dealer and asked the man how much it would set me back to put a tire on my truck. After taking one look at my tires, he smirked and said, "You don't have a decent tire on the rig. You need four new tires."

"I didn't ask what I needed," I snapped. "I asked you how much one tire would cost me." I have eyes, I knew I needed four tires and a whole lot more for that old truck, but I was pretty sure I had enough money for one tire.

A few days later, Randy showed up for his hunt with four new tires in the back of his truck. I appreciated that, but that was not what I wanted. I wanted the landowners to be stand-up people, and I wanted them to do what they say and say what they do.

In my heart I knew Randy was right. I knew that faith in my Heavenly Father shouldn't depend on one of the biggest corporations in the world. I just couldn't give up. My family and I had put every last dime we had made into cleaning up this pit. We had spent our own money to put in a yard and we built beautiful ponds. We completely remodeled the house, and we hauled off what seemed like hundreds of truckloads of accumulated garbage and junk. We had taken down miles of broken-down fence and installed a new sprinkler system.

We cleaned ditches that hadn't been touched in years, and slowly brought back life to the fields. We built sporting clay and archery ranges. The business was booming, and after almost twenty years of struggle, we were finally getting there. We had six more years left on our lease agreement. My lawyer estimated we would be giving up over two million dollars of gross income. Randy yawned as I passionately listed my losses.

"A couple million dollars is a lot of money to a dog trainer, Randy," I said.

"I know it is, Mike," he countered, "but I also know the value of what you have. You cannot beat them in a court battle. They have dozens of hand-picked lawyers on staff, and the suit won't cost them a dime or a minute's sleep."

He was right, of course, he was right.

Randy sat on the back of his car and laid his shotgun across his lap. I was pacing back and forth with Sally on my waist cord and just couldn't settle down. I was losing everything I'd worked for, and he calmly said "So what."

He thoughtfully picked at his shooting gloves, and after a time asked me to just listen to him for a minute. I was agitated, for sure, but because of my deep respect for Randy I relented and knelt down on one knee to hear what he had to say.

"As you know, Mike, I love to sail," he began. "I've sailed around the world in my own ship. My wife and children probably spent more time sailing than they did on dry land. My kids were practically raised at sea. One time we sailed into some terrifically high seas. We were fighting for our very lives. I had to stay awake for two days and man the ship until we could break out of the storm. What do you think my primary concern was during those two days?"

"Well, of course, the safety of your family," I answered.

"Do you think it would have mattered much if one of my companies' executives had contacted me on the ship-to-shore radio and told me that I had just lost a couple million dollars that day? Do you think that would've changed my priorities?"

"No," I said.

"My priority was simple. Get my family safely out of that dilemma, and that's what I did. And Mike," he said deliberately, "get yours out of this one."

We hunted the rest of the year knowing it would be our last. My problems became trivial and meaningless when Randy's daughter Gaylen was diagnosed with bone cancer. She was the same age as me.

As I would expect, Randy stiffened under the pressure and Jody tried everything she could to make Gaylen comfortable. It seemed only a few months until Holly and I were standing on the hill above Randy's house while friends and family remembered a person that meant so much to them.

I quit struggling after that and faced my demise.

I was injured and weak. It was hard to believe that such a gallant effort was to be recorded as a failure. My spirit was leaving me as my creditors circled overhead.

I was offered a job in Idaho managing a big hunting club. Randy insisted I take Sally along. Maybe someday we could get together up there. I don't remember our last hunt together in Colorado, the three of us.

I packed up and headed north. The plan was for me to work for a couple of months to get our feet under us, and then return for the family and our stuff. I was less than enthusiastic, because this project had all the earmarks of my next drubbing.

After a time, I found a place for us to live and headed on home to get the family. I left my dogs at the new ranch under the care of the staff. Even though I gave them strict orders as to how I wanted the dogs care for, I was greeted home with the news of Sally's death. The trainer calmly said everything went well except for one old dog dying. I looked him square in the eyes and asked him to repeat himself. My teeth were clenched so tightly I could feel them breaking.

"Oh, you know, that old shorthair," he said offhandedly. "She died a couple of days ago."

"What the hell happened to her?" I hissed. "She was feeling fine when I left."

"I don't know," he said casually. "The vet said it had something to do with her stomach."

"What vet?" I growled.

I found out that Sally had died of gastric torsion. It may have been that she died naturally, but I should have been there. I called Randy with the news. There wasn't much to say. I think I felt worse than he did.

I didn't talk to Randy for a year or so after that, but I was excited when he called to reserve a hunt with me in the upcoming fall. He was to drive all the way to Idaho for a two-day hunt. He planned to bring his son Barry along.

We were busy again, setting up hunts, fishing trips and dog training. There was only one hunt I cared about. After my last hunt with Randy in Colorado, I decided not to guide any more hunts. I had plenty of young guys on my staff and I had trained them to handle the dogs and the clientele. I brought my dog team up and installed them into the daily routine of the bird hunting program, and they were handling the lion's share of the hunts.

I warned the staff far in advance of Randy's arrival that I would be handling his hunt and his accommodations. I knew he wouldn't put up with any funny stuff. I chose Jay Daniels, a young dog handler, to help me with Randy. Jay was a delight to work with. He had no preconceived notions about bird hunting and was not the least bit arrogant or presumptuous. Jay had a wonderful bright smile, and I knew I could depend on him.

I had bred and raised a superb English pointer I called Harrier. Harrier was a splendid bird dog in every respect, and was the stellar performer of the ranch team.

I had assigned him to Jay, because I knew he would take good care of Jay until he learned the ropes. Harrier had the ability to keep Jay out of trouble until Jay learned to recognize it for himself.

Harrier reminded me a lot of Sally in his application of work ethic. He was beautiful to watch and easy to handle. I knew he would do the job at hand, and I knew Randy would appreciate his talent.

Sure enough, Randy and Barry showed up on time. It was great to see them. I had met Barry once before, down at my old place in Colorado. After greeting Holly and I, Randy asked to see his room. I could tell he was tired from the drive and wanted to relax.

It was late in the afternoon, but still an hour or so away from our regular dinner time at the lodge. Normally the kitchen staff would prepare some sort of an appetizer and hors d'oeuvre tray for the guests to warm up on while they were changing out of their hunting clothes and getting ready for the evening. We had just hired an ex-airline stewardess as an office helpmate, and she had taken it upon herself to bring the tray down to the sitting room.

The other guests in the lodge were still out hunting and we expected them to be working their way back soon. A couple of the guests were in their rooms and had requested some appetizers to be brought up to them—I guess they thought they were more important than the others.

This flaunting misfit of a waitress waved the tray in front of Randy and Barry, but before they could commit to a selection, she swept it into the hallway toward the lower rooms.

Randy sat there for a moment and then decided to go home. He was not one to stand for that kind of a slight, and besides that, he was hungry. He'd been driving for a long while, and was looking forward to something decent to eat. He sat down his cocktail and headed for his bedroom. He asked Holly if she knew anywhere in town where he could get something to eat. He wasn't kidding. He was leaving.

Randy always loved Holly and she was able to smooth things over for him that evening before I cornered the culprit in the office and threatened her life. "If you so much as look at him again, I'll run you off the ranch for good," I told her.

"I'll just go explain what happened," she curtly hissed in her best, sugar-sweet-ex-whatever-she-was voice.

"Just stay away from him," I warned her.

The next morning was beautiful. I drove a custom-built hunting jeep with Randy sitting on the passenger side. Barry and Jay rode in the elevated rear seats above Harrier and his bracemate.

Jay casted the dogs into a pretty sloping field we had planted in fescue, wheat grass, and alfalfa. The dogs were flying across their ground and Randy was grinning from ear to ear. Suddenly the dogs slammed into a couple of Hungarian partridge, who flushed wildly and sped off into the distance.

"What were those?" Randy asked.

"Huns," I told him. "We will probably see plenty of them this morning."

Randy carried his twenty-eight gauge at port arms and I walked closely alongside, just like old times. I was holding his walking stick. I knew we would soon be trading. Barry walked above us with Randy's matching twenty cradled in his arms.

Harrier spun into the wind and came down hard as he looked into some lodging winter wheat. As Randy closed in, Jay put the bird to wing and Randy's second barrel brought him down.

My heart was light, like the feathers that drifted in the Idaho morning mist. The ever-present early fog lay heavy in the Lawyer Creek drainage, and the sun glowed through to reveal Harrier's bracemate, Jake, carrying the bird.

Randy turned to me and said, "Well, that's enough for me this morning. Mike, you take one, and we will let Jay and Barry hunt the remainder of the day."

I reached out for his shotgun and extended his walking stick to him. Even this insignificant act meant so much to me on this very special morning.

After I was successful in holding up my end of the deal, Randy and I spent the rest of the outing riding in the jeep and taking pictures. For the first time, he had brought a video camera along and he was recording the events as they unfolded.

Jay and Barry were out front, and both gave us ample opportunity to give them grief over their respective misses. We laughed at their excuses. Jay was able to convert his very-first-ever double on Huns, and Randy quickly piled out of the jeep to take his picture. I don't know Barry very well, but he seemed to be enjoying his morning, also.

The birds were plentiful, and soon Randy asked for a count. Jay tallied them and reported back. "You can each shoot one more, and then we're done for the day, okay?" Randy said.

We soon collected the last pair, and were loading gear into the jeep for the trip back to the lodge. I looked up the hill and saw Harrier and Jake holding a huge covey of Huns. The birds were anxiously settled into some sparse cover near a wide strip of mowed grass.

Both Jay and Barry started for the pointing dogs before Randy reminded them the hunt was over. Jay look puzzled for a moment, then smiled broadly and gathered up his dogs. Randy liked Jay—I knew he would. Jay will accompany hundreds of shooters in his guiding career, but he will never forget that morning, or that man.

The next morning was a close replica of the first, only we saw more pheasant than the first day. Randy always preferred to hunt pheasant, and he wouldn't shoot a bobwhite quail if you showed him a thousand. He just didn't feel right shooting them.

Harrier was spectacular on the second morning. I was so proud of him. He just stayed in the birds. He handled them like he knew how important it was to me.

Somehow I felt different that day. It seemed to be a finality of sorts. I can't explain the attitude that slowly crept to me and chilled my soul. "Could this time be the last?" I thought. "Will I never again experience the honor of lending my arm in support? Will I never trade his walking stick for the shotgun, then wait patiently until the trade was reversed and complete?"

I wondered to myself how the Colonel felt. I wondered if this day meant as much to him. I knew he didn't drive eleven hundred miles just to shoot two pheasant. I sensed he wanted to see for himself how my family and I were making out.

While driving toward the lodge, we passed grassy fields and thick holdings of hawthorne and wild rose. We drove into the water of Lawyer Creek and ground across the volcanic bed while the jeep creaked and winced.

Jay and Barry laughed as they recounted the morning's tale. I accommodated their rendition, then stared and grasped for composure.

I thought of Noose and old Jake Taylor. I suddenly recalled Jack O'Brien and his rambling stories of the freight trains. I'd recently heard that Jim Darien suffered a heart attack on Main Street in Carbondale and died less than one block from where I'd seen him last.

I wondered if my dad would've been proud of me and what I've accomplished. I thought of Bill Tarrant as I shivered to the humid chill of Idaho's autumn. This damp weather would be hard on him, I thought, I hoped he was somewhere warm today.

Randy was traveling light. It didn't take him long to throw his duffle into the Subaru and say his goodbyes. I watched him drive away, then retreated to my upstairs office to part the blinds and look where he had gone.

All of a sudden it occurred to me, he never did give me the twenty bucks. He did give generously to my family each Christmas, and he was always leaving books of poetry. He gave us three shotguns and a rare rifle. My son Bryce won three All-American titles with one of the shotguns, and my son Jayme won the only tournament he ever entered with the other. He gave me sweaters and hunting vests, shirts and hats—heck, I was still holding the shirt and vest he had worn while hunting today. Once he gave me $500 toward a wedding ring for Holly after she had to hock her first one to keep us in business. He patiently offered business advice and support. Many of the things Randy gave us were very valuable, but he would always say, "I had this lying around, you can have it if you can use it."

Randy gave me friendship and then taught me the value of it.

Some of the other hunters were starting to come into the lodge, so I shook it off and headed downstairs to meet them. I followed a couple of excited shooters into the gun room to listen to their story of the morning. I was leaning against the gun-cleaning table while they were waving their arms and pulling off their hunting jackets.

They were frantically pointing at each other and were cracking good-natured jokes about each other's shooting. They complimented the dog work and the guides. "Everything was great, everything was great, just perfect," they beamed.

Suddenly I caught a glimpse of something white sitting on top of the cleaning bench. I reached up and pulled down two plastic cottage cheese containers. One was about half full of light 7½ shot, and the other held 6's.

There were also two biscuits for Sally.

About a week later I received a large portrait of Sally. The note from Randy said, "Hang it in a place of honor."

I'll do that, Colonel Blatz... I will indeed.

There are few things more perfect than a flower,
There may only be but one.
There are few things more lovely,
I can only think of one.
Could it be the sparkle in the heavens,
When all your world seems dark,
Or the fortune, cast in starlight,
For he who wins your heart.

The Flower at My Feet

Damn, I was tired. Coyotes kept my dogs going most of the night, and half a dozen elk ran through camp somewhere in the middle of it. I had been walking in a steady rain for over five miles. I had finally given up on keeping anything dry, and from the looks of it, the weather didn't have any intention of making it better for me. It wasn't too bad, really—the temperature was hanging in there at about 55 or 60 degrees, and, lacking a wind to move it one way or the other, the rain was falling straight from heaven to earth.

I was running two flashy pointer girls who had yet to come up with a water-loving covey this morning. They had run a great reaching race, but each of them had clearly enjoyed about all of this they could stand. They would occasionally break out of the dense, rolling fog to show me they were still handling, still hunting...still trying.

This is the kind of storm that just lays on you. There's no telling where it came from, or where it's going. I knew it was moving fairly rapidly, because I could follow the swirling clouds of fog as they embraced the mountain for a short time and then moved on without looking back.

Patches of timber looked worried as they were consumed by

this strange daytime darkness. Suddenly they were reassured as they once again caught a glimpse of their likeness across the park.

I decided to sit down on a big rock and wait for the dogs to cast around to me. I was instantly reminded of another day when the weather was much worse, but you couldn't tell it by the grouse that were congregated out in the parks.

It was the opening day of grouse season, the second Saturday in September 1989. My boys and I were camped with Gary Ruppel and several of our friends at a camp we call "Hungry Bear, Wine Women." Strange name, huh? Well, here's how it came by it.

One day I was runing three black Labrador males between Willow Springs and Tie Gulch. We were on our way down the mountain and only stopped there to get one last hunt in before heading for home. There was a group of fishermen camped just inside the timber, on the edge of a big park of stunted sagebrush, one of our favorite grouse-hunting haunts.

Actually, I didn't know the fishermen were there until I came out of the timber and ran into them on a well-used deer trail. All of them looked like they had just seen a ghost. One older fellow, with about a three-day stand of beard stubble, was shaking like a quakie leaf. They were studying some cellophane wrappers and picking up some trash that had been scattered along the trail.

"Where'd you come from?" one of them squeaked. I think he was getting a little mad and I still hadn't figured out what the heck was going on.

"I've been working dogs down off the peak there," I said as I pointed up the hill. "We're scouting for blue grouse."

"Oh, those were dogs?" he asked, his voice quavering.

"Yeah, I'm running three Labs," I replied.

They all let out a breath and started muttering to each other while I walked up to them. "Didn't mean to scare you," I said politely. "I didn't know anyone was camped over here."

One guy finally spoke up to let me in on what was bothering them so much. He showed me a crunched-up meat wrapper and a handful of torn packages and styrofoam containers. "We just had a big black bear raid our camp. He ransacked our cooler and all our grub. We have been fishing up at Heart Lake for a few days, and we don't even have a gun with us, so we stayed in the tent until we couldn't hear him outside any longer."

About that time my dogs came hustling up to us to see what was keeping me. The men all looked at them like they wanted to kill 'em and cook their skulls.

"We were trailing the bear," the guy continued, "picking up our meat packages, when those dogs of yours came blasting down the trail and sent us all looking for a tree to climb. Goddammit, my heart is still pounding. Those dogs scared the pie out of us."

"I'm sure sorry, friend," I said, "I hope they didn't take any years off of any of you folks." I started walking up and down the trail until I got a good look at the bear's track. "You're right, he was a dandy, and if you scared him half as bad as he did you, he's making it for the low country. Poor bear, he'll probably never recover. I'm damn sure glad you folks weren't hunting. You'd have filled those dogs of mine plumb full of holes."

"You can be sure of that," one fellow laughed. "Them ol' dogs of yours would be tits up right now if I had anything that resembled a gun with me."

"You don't mind if I put 'em on a lead while we walk back to your camp, do you?" I asked. "It's not that I don't trust you, but maybe one of you guys might seek some kind of revenge yet."

We sat around their camp for a while and laughed about the whole ordeal. It must have been something to see three black beasts charge from the woods while you're standing on a fresh bear track with nothing but hamburger in your hands.

It might be hard to believe, but "Wine Women" is actually a term of endearment. It reminds us of someone very beautiful and very special.

Gary Ruppel and his family love to dedicate a few days each fall to a family outing while Gary works his dogs. Gary's wife, Kathy, can turn a little clearing in the quakies into a full-service five-star hotel. She is in perpetual motion as she works off of her own private blueprint. She leans a pole up there, props a rope up here, hangs an awning here, sets a table there. I've seen her lay pine boughs to keep the dust down around her custom-made benches.

She hums and laughs her way through the day, stopping occasionally to pick flower arrangements, play with her daughter, or simply admire the meadows. I've been in plenty of camps in my time, but Kathy's is the only one I make sure to wipe my feet before entering.

It just so happens that Gary and Kathy chose to set up their training camp in the exact same location the fishermen had set up theirs.

Now, Kathy isn't what I would call a drinker. Oh, she enjoys a little wine every now and then, but it's not like she makes a career out of it or anything. She is very structured and reasonable, it's good to have her around; it gives us all something to shoot for.

On this trip, Kathy brought along a bottle of special wine. I never saw it, but I suspect it was a big one. Like I say, I wasn't there, but for some reason she decided to put the hurt on that thing.

You have to know, there isn't a flat spot anywhere near that particular camp. The whole thing is on a slant. That could've had something to do with the damage ol' Kathy did to herself that night. One thing about it, there ain't a bear in his right mind who woulda tried that camp for the next couple of days. She'd a beat him to a pulp and then run him clear off the mountain.

Well, that's why we call it "Hungry Bear, Wine Women Camp," and it's one of our favorites.

We were sitting around the fire the night before grouse season opened in 1989 when one of those early-season storms ripped into us. We turned in early, hoping the winds would take it well beyond the divide before morning.

Some of the hunters flat refused to poke their noses out of their sleeping bags at the alarm, because you could hear the tent flapping, and hard, hail-like pellets of snow were popping the canvas in a steady beat. I told my boys to stay inside. "Gary and I are going to give it a look," I said. "I doubt if we will be out there for long."

I think four of us ended up loading a few dogs and ourselves into the truck for the short ride over to the rim. It was one of those times where you can't think about it too long. You either do it, or you don't. Either way it has to happen, now.

We jumped out in the park above the overlook and leaned into a fierce west wind that was driving BB-sized snowflakes horizontally across the tall grass. I couldn't breathe at first without turning my head to the side. I put on my sunglasses to protect my eyes from the stinging snow. The idea was to make a quick run through the park, and if nothing was happening, we would retreat back to camp until the storm blew over.

We all loved to hunt grouse, but this was bordering on ridiculous. My collar was zipped to the top, and my gloves were freezing around my shotgun. I hoped my chaps would turn the snow for at least an hour before they caved in to the pressure.

None of us were prepared for what we saw. The grouse coveys were out feeding like it was the Fourth of July. They were soaked to the bone, but they were out there, and it didn't seem like they minded the weather much. Maybe when you live so close to the ground, the wind doesn't bother you like it does everyone else. I don't know. I only know that there were grouse in the park that day, and when they got up, the wind cranked them into a dive that made it almost impossible to get a pattern on them.

As I sat on the rock, waiting for my dogs, I vividly remembered that morning, and how astonishing it was that the birds were casually feeding. I shivered and pulled my gloves on tight. Just thinking about that morning made me want to build a fire.

On a number of occasions, I've seen dramatic dog work on sage grouse when it was raining so hard you could hardly see. I don't mean that slow, romantic, misty drizzle; I'm talking about big drops that pop the bill of your hat so hard, you have to keep adjusting it to keep it on.

Twice, while guiding in south Texas, I sloshed through mean-tempered rain that stayed on for over a week and had everyone along the coast looking for higher ground. The grumpy top-level executives I was guiding even quit complaining about their poor choice of weekends as they witnessed the work of some amazingly talented bird dogs.

They leaned expensive shotguns in the corners of swank lodges, while their soaked hunting clothes were hanging off of deer antlers and door knobs, kitchen chairs and coat racks. They sat around the fireplace and toasted to the mud-caked, hard-working pointers who dug out the coveys that made it all worthwhile.

I grinned to myself as I recalled those hunts in standing water that had the quail on their tip-toes. Both of the dogs I had with me on this day had spent two seasons in Texas, and even though I hadn't seen them in quite a spell now, I knew they were out there trying to make something happen.

We were just above Oval Spring, on a south-facing slope that gently comes out from under you and stretches out below. Although I couldn't see either, I knew there were three small patches of quakies just off to my right, and a quick little drop-off into some scattered timber on my left. I kept searching the hazy edges of the park for the tiniest glimpse of a bird dog.

The rain seemed to intensify, and plump clouds of fog the color of pine smoke gathered around me. Sometimes the best thing to do is nothing. If the dogs were still running, they'd find me. Even if they got tangled up with some deer or elk, they wouldn't be distracted long. Neither one of these dogs were bad for running off game. If the birds didn't get jumpy or the dogs impatient, I'd find them both together.

I remembered the time I was running a pretty little setter over by the main road. Some people from Denver saw her run across the road, so they figured she must be lost and needed saving. They loaded her up and took her home. She was missing just over two weeks before I finally got her rounded up.

That was not going to happen today. First of all, I didn't think there was anyone nearby, and secondly, stopping to pick up a clean, fluffy setter is one thing. Asking two muddy, rain-soaked pointers to hop into your car is a whole different ballgame.

I not only settled with my situation, I was starting to thoroughly enjoy it. It's not often a guy can just sit and think without the sights and sounds of a busy world. I've spent most of my life in these mountains, and I'm used to gazing out across them as I drift and dream. Now it was as if they didn't even exist. Isn't it funny...although my world was suddenly very small, and my vision was confined to a few feet, my spirit was challenged to focus and appreciate what was there?

One fall in Idaho I was guiding a delightful man from Arkansas.

His attitude was so upbeat—he was cordial and friendly to the other guests, and he always put the cheerful spin on every single thing that happened while he was with me. He was so uplifting to be around, and he had a terrific smile that would flash at the drop of a hat. He hadn't just won the lottery or anything; he wasn't even wealthy. He was a career helicopter pilot who had saved for three years to come on this bird hunting trip.

On the second morning of our hunt together, I decided to tell him how much I appreciated his overall demeanor. While we were taking a mid-morning break, I noticed him standing behind the dog truck. He was drinking a cup of coffee as he looked out over the mountains. He was laughing to himself and smiled big when he saw me coming over. "Hell of a day, isn't it?" he said.

"It sure is," I replied, "and you're making it better for all of us."

"Well, thanks for saying so, but the way I figure it, I can't make the days any shorter, longer, or better...I can only make them worse," he said thoughtfully. "A long time ago, I made a deal with myself: I'm making the most of every day I'm lucky enough to wake up to. Basically, that's the long and the short of it."

"Well, I can tell you for sure, my friend, you've brightened up my week. I've been guiding nearly every day for several months now, and the grind was taking its toll. Just meeting you has given me the inspiration to finish the season," I said, wanting to make sure he knew how I felt.

"I haven't always been this way," he confided. "When I was young, I was very excitable and jumpy. I couldn't sit still for five minutes. When I was in my teens, I was a little devil. Looking back, I feel sorry for my parents.

"When I was in my twenties, I was flying low. I was moving so fast I didn't dare think about what I was passing. One day I went by something that looked like a red blur.

"In my thirties, I had slowed a little, but as I blew by that same spot, I noticed that it was both red and green. I still didn't give it much thought.

"While in my forties, I could easily see something red on a green bush. I was now more interested in what it was, but still did not slow down enough check it out.

"One day, while in my mid-fifties, I was walking down the same path and I was finally able to identify it. It was a red flower on a green bush.

"I'm now in my sixties, and my favorite pastime is to sit beside that green bush and smell those red flowers. It took me fifty years to finally slow down enough to appreciate what I was passing by every day. Now ain't that something?"

I put my hand on the back of his neck. "It sure is, sir," I said. "It truly is."

As I recalled the story of the hunter from Arkansas, I found myself looking around the base of the rock I was sitting on. I leaned over, reached down, and picked a purple fringe phacelia. Water poured off my jacket sleeve and temporarily flattened the delicate petals. I held the flower to my nose and breathed as deep as I could—I was sure glad I met that fellow.

I hated to move, but it had been over half an hour since I'd seen my dogs. If I could get within fifty yards of them, I might be able to make them out, I thought. I didn't really have a clue as to which direction they were, so I felt the best plan was to check two nearby locations that I knew had been holding coveys.

Blue grouse don't really stray much. If the food source stays in there for them, they will generally be close to where you saw them last. "Well, one thing's for sure, water isn't a problem for them today," I laughed to myself.

I started downhill with the idea being to make a big circle that would end up in the three patches of quakies that were still buried somewhere out in that fog. Every now and then I could make out an old limb sticking up or a rock outcropping. I walked slowly and studied everything as carefully as I could. A long, meandering line of scattered timber started to materialize as I approached. I knew I was just above a small water hole that was surrounded by watercress, willows and chokecherries. There were times when we'd manage to get a covey pointed on the edge of those willows, so I skirted the brush while trying to stay about fifty yards out in the park.

I knew the dogs would trail me if they happened to come back around while I was down there, so I didn't have to look behind me. After several false alarms, I reached the lower end of the trees and looked hard out into the haze for anything moving.

I don't like to try to guess where a dog might have gone. I'm just not that good at it, but I didn't have any choice today. I curled into the rolling thickness and started along the sidehill toward the quakies. I walked a little, listened a little, walked a little, listened a little until I felt sure that I was somewhere just below the three quakie patches. There was a decent covey that hung out up there, and my hope was that my dogs were keeping them company until I could get in on it.

Quakies trees are white. They're a lot harder to see in heavy fog than evergreens. I felt like I was looking through wax paper. I could walk within seventy-five yards of those trees and maybe never see them.

Gradually, vague shapes started to appear just to my left. "Whew, it's about time," I sighed. I was coming into the lower patch, and now I knew exactly where I was.

When you spend most of your time looking at wildlife, you learn to look for things different, things that don't go along with a natural setting. Many times you will notice an odd color in the oak brush long before you finally identify it as a bull elk. You look for motion, something out of place, something that, for some reason, just doesn't belong there.

That's what I saw in the middle of that patch of quakies—something different. Three connected dark spots, each a little larger than a softball. A new wave of fog briefly blew between us, so I stood quietly and stared into it where I had just seen the spots seconds before.

As the spots once again took shape, I slowly walked toward them until I saw another. This time I knew what it was—Silk's head. Elhew Silkwood is a white-and-liver pointer with several large body spots on both sides. I still couldn't make out her outline, but I recognized her spot pattern. It was her for sure.

She had a habit of stretching one leg out front and sort of kneeling down on the other when she pointed while going downhill.

Generally when she pointed like this, her head would be either straight out or slightly lower than her front shoulder. This time her head was very high.

"Bet you were wondering where I've been, baby," I softly spoke to her. "I hope you're as glad to see me as I am to see you."

I started to her front while keeping an eye in the direction she was looking. It was then I realized why she was holding her head so high. She wasn't pointing, she was backing. Her bracemate, Grand River Satin, is nearly all white. She had a pretty liver mask, but beings how she was pointing directly away from me, there was absolutely no way I could have seen her. Even after I knew she was there, I couldn't really separate her from the surrounding grayness. She felt my presence and inched ahead a foot or so.

"Whoup," I whispered. "Nice job, kid. You're so pretty."

I circled to the front as quickly as I could and started toward Satin's head. There was a dead quakie log lying diagonally in front of her, and just beyond that a little clump of mountain mahogany. Snowberry bushes crowded around the front of several big rocks, and that's where I found the grouse. First the hen went, along with two birds of the year.

Both dogs jumped forward a few feet.

"Whoa, whoup," I said, as I held my drenched glove in the air so they could see it. I knew there were six birds in this covey, but it was possible half of them had already bailed on us. I didn't really think that was the

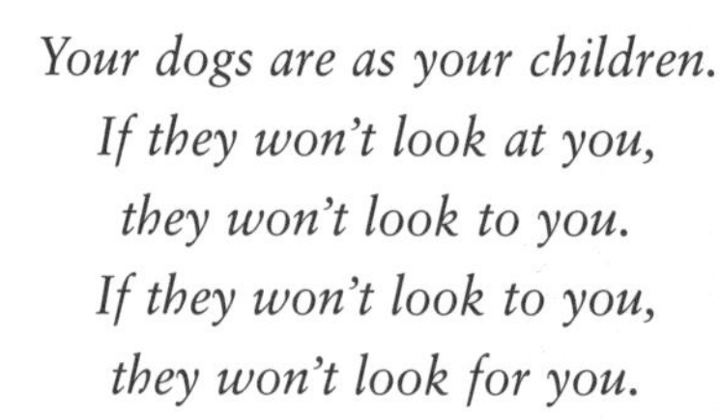

Your dogs are as your children.
If they won't look at you,
they won't look to you.
If they won't look to you,
they won't look for you.

case, because the hen wouldn't have set still while three of her brood flew off without her. I found them twenty yards distant, casually walking up the hill.

All three of us stood and watched the last three birds disappear into the mist. God, that was beautiful.

"C'mere, you guys," I called to my dogs. "I don't know if I've ever been prouder of you." They were cold, both of them shivering as they stood there. Their ears were drooping and their eyes had that sad puppy-dog look.

I pulled my waist cords from around my shoulder and slipped one on each of them. We walked together to the top of the rim and caught the Chelldavia Trail toward camp. I knelt down and gave them each a big squeeze of Nutri-Cal to keep their energy up. I didn't want hypothermia to set in, and I'm sure they didn't either.

We walked side by side into the black timber of Dead Horse Point and followed the trail we knew would take us home. We couldn't see twenty yards to either side as we strolled and talked for two-and-a-half hours.

When wet turns to cold, the knees start to stiffen and feet become more sensitive to their ground. Stepping over logs awakens tired thigh muscles and causes cold chaps to press tight against the legs.

We only saw one covey that day, but that seemed like enough. What a great and glorious find. What a splendid moment in life. It was a day in which we were encased in a smaller world than we're used to. This was a magical hunt, a mysterious, moody picture of faith that called me to use my direction within. My long walk into that dense fog was unsuccessful, even as I slowed my pace to closer study my footing. Finally, beneath an unyielding shroud, I realized a remarkable opportunity to admire a tiny red flower, blooming at my feet.

Now ain't that something?

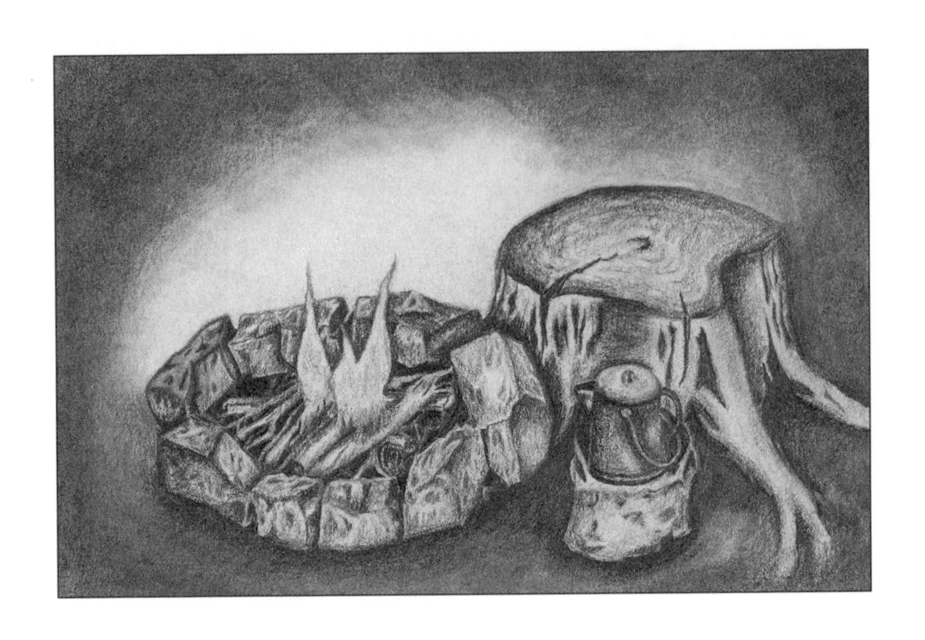

The essence of life: Earth, wind, fire, water...and coffee.

A Day with the Firemaster

WHOOOMF! The ceiling of my make-shift tent was aglow. I knew it was getting close to five a.m. The dogs had been sparring and growling for half an hour or so. The glow on my ceiling was a reflection of the campfire that Danny Watson had just torched. I had come to expect it every morning, and every morning it came.

We had constructed the tent to cover our dog box. It looked more like a car port, or a single-car garage, than it did a tent. We had found a four-inch piece of foam that matched the dimensions of the box and turned it into the best bed I've ever had in the mountains.

The dogs slept below us, so we could easily keep them quiet through the night, and we could stop any wrestling or growling matches that broke out.

Each morning we hustled to load the dogs onto the chain gang as the coffeepot gurgled and hissed on the fire. Usually it would boil over while we were involved with our chores. Then we'd both dash to yank the volcanic pot from the fire. You have to be careful when you grab a coffeepot out of the fire. It can put a mark on your glove that it will never forget. I think every man I know has tried to do it barehanded—once. It's like the old hunting camp story about shooting off horses. The question was always, "Can I shoot off of this horse?" and the reply was simple: "Yeah...once." Some things don't need further explanation.

Danny started the fire every morning. It was like a ritual to him. He learned the art from his grandfather. It wasn't an ancient method of rubbing sticks or exact kindling arrangement. It was more the result of a cup of Coleman fuel, one match, and quick reflexes. I think the quick reflexes were the hardest thing to get down pat. I'm sure there were some singed eyebrows and arm hair along the road to perfection of the family secret.

I affectionately nicknamed him "The Firemaster." It seemed to suit him.

The test of campfire coffee isn't in the making of it as much as in the drinking of it. The last couple of cups in the pot can get pretty "meaty," if you know what I mean. While running our dogs, we would always pick some wild licorice heads to drop in the mix. It gives coffee a unique taste.

This morning was just like all the rest. We sipped our brew with one hand while we scooped dog pucky with the other. After the chores had been taken care of, we sat together at the fire and talked about our plans for the day.

Today I was going to make the two-hour drive down to town to try and pry some money out of our training clients. Several of them had promised to go to the hip for us today, and we were down to our last few dollars. We were both seining our gear for gas money. Danny would tend the camp and work the dogs while I did the bowing and scraping.

Today also promised an additional attraction—I was invited to meet with a developer who was willing to consider our dog-training program on some land he had purchased. For some reason, he had decided to delay the destruction of one of the prettiest river bottoms in Colorado for a year or so while he drummed up support for his golf complex.

"Good luck," Danny hollered. "Have a good day."

"Yeah, you do the same," I said, as I jumped a couple of pups into the front seat of the truck and eased out of camp. It was just getting daylight. I didn't have time to hunt on the way down, but if

I caught a covey of grouse in the road, I could put the pups on them without losing much time.

Sunlight streamed across the back side of Coyote Park as I swung out of the timber and headed to the west. Both of the pups were staring hard through the window. They were young, but this wasn't their first trip down. They knew we would be looking for anything moving.

The lurching truck helps to develop anti-coffee spilling skills. I don't know why I always have to bring a cup with me; I almost always spill half of it, and end up throwing the last little bit out the window in frustration.

This morning routine was nothing new. Danny and I had been on the road most of the year. We had logged in over 25,000 miles hauling our team across the West. We had spent the entire spring working the Lolo Creek drainage in northern Idaho. We walked every old logging skid and game trail between the Musselshell and Lolo Creek. For weeks we explored the lower Maggie Butte area around an old sawmill the locals called "Haystries."

Although there were many hound men up in that country, we were the only bird dog trainers working within a hundred miles. We frequently found lost hounds and hauled them around until we ran into the owners. They never did quite figure out what we were doing up there. I know they joked about it amongst themselves. One old hound man made fun of our dogs when he saw us drive right past a big cougar in the road, and not one of them struck. He told one of his friends, who just happened to know us, "Those old boys aren't going to catch a damn thing. They drove right by that cougar and none of those sorry dogs of theirs caught a nose-full. Why, I wouldn't even feed that lot."

His friend laughed as he broke the news. "Those aren't hounds, those are bird dogs."

We camped up Sweetwater Creek, near Glenwood Springs, Colorado, for a couple of weeks in June. Our pups were really growing at that time, and we were starting to outgrow our dog quarters. We were carrying 23 altogether, including pups and adult dogs.

After a quick trip back to Idaho, we set up down on the Colorado River. We stayed there until the end of June, then we moved our camp to the high country. We had been there a couple of months and winter would be coming on pretty soon. We were working hard to find a new place where we could set up for a time.

I was driving slowly, glimpsing the breaks above Broken Rib Bottoms, when I suddenly felt the dogs get intense. Both of them were leaning forward, looking through the windshield.

There was a calf elk loping down the road about 75 yards in front of us. I followed her for a short while before she dropped down over a rise; she wasn't all that worried. I turned the truck off and coasted toward the spot where I'd last seen her. We barely had enough speed to make the rise, so we were creeping along without making much noise when we topped out to see the timber in front of us. Elk started moving everywhere. That's the way it is with elk, you're either miles away from them, or you're right in the middle of them.

The dogs whined as I counted. "I got 48," I whispered to them. The elk were melting into the timber toward a little saddle where I used to camp years ago. I called that camp "Hidden Coffee Camp." I used to keep an old coffeepot hidden in the underbrush near the spring there. When I happened by there with my grouse-hunting clients, we would often stop for a cup.

When I couldn't see any more elk, I started the truck and headed into the switchbacks above the bottoms. The road makes a big swing around Broken Rib Bottoms because it is very boggy and thick with alders. We broke out of the timber just at the edge of the bog and the sprawling parks above Grizzly Creek were just catching their first rays. Off to my right I saw six bull elk standing together. They had just crossed the road before me and were surprised to see me coming down the road at that time of the morning.

They were all nice, branch-antlered bulls. Two four-points, and four five-points. Now, you don't see that every day. They were standing tall as their necks stretched to test the wind. They were all in velvet; the antlers look so much bigger when they're all fuzzy and backlit. It was nice to see so many elk this close to camp. They seem to be strangely attracted to the dogs. I know they are similarly attracted to horses, and likewise.

I could sit and watch elk all day, but I had an appointment or two to make. I slowly drove away from the bulls as they stood on the ridge and followed my leaving.

I was greatly inspired as I gazed out toward the Grizzly Creek Canyon while chest-high lupine, larkspur, wild geranium, and shrubby cinquefoil scratched at the sides of the truck. I reached out and squeezed passing flower blossoms in my glove until the leather was wet with fragrance.

This was part of the famous Ute Trail. I could only guess the Indians stopped at Broken Rib Spring, so I paid homage as I stopped there to fill my water bottle and breathe deep as I scanned the east-facing rim of the canyon. Many times there were mule deer feeding along those radical slopes, but it took some looking to get them spotted, at least for me.

The Utes called this place "The Land of the Shining Mountains."

On many mountains, my foot prints were the only proof
Of my ever having been there. But on the rim above
Broken Rib Spring, I left a little more than that.
A fallen warrior, a brother—He was my vision
of greatness, Now, my fondest memory.

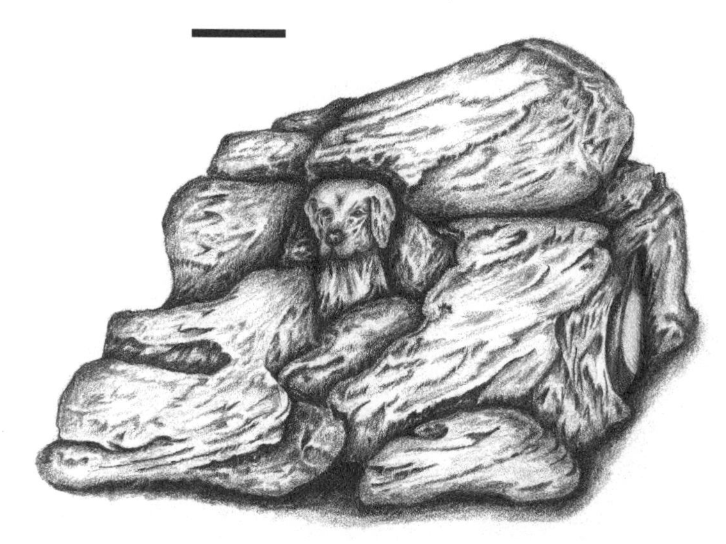

They must have decided upon that name while sitting here...while drinking this water...while breathing this air. These mountains not only shine with the early light of day, they shine with life, and hope. They inspire you to take up your burden and strike out for the next hill, to keep on when the trail is uncertain. Isn't that the essence of faith, to reach when the handhold isn't visible, to step when the footing is obsure?

The road below the spring is well traveled, so I reluctantly picked up speed. I couldn't spend all morning up here. I still had a long drive to Aspen. "You guys keep a lookout for grouse, will you?" I talked to the dogs because they were starting to cozy to the glaring sun as it warmed the cab and begged them to snooze. "Pretty soon we'll be down on the highway. There won't be much to see from there on out, so why don't you plan on doing your sleeping then?"

I suspect there is at least one particular angel in charge of arranging the scenery of the Rockies. I sometimes wish I knew his name. I just wish I could thank him personally. His work has stirred my soul and permanently glazed my spirit. If my eyes grew dark at this very instant, to never again see the light of day, I could rest assured that I could recall its every detail. That which I could not see, I could smell. That which I could not smell, I could hear. And that which I could not hear, I could feel.

My heart was bright with emotion as the pups and I broke out on the rim to start the 5,000-foot descent to the valley floor. For the next fifteen miles, the road fairly clings to the edge of the canyon wall until its dizzying raft of switchbacks drops you at the confluence of Deep Creek and the Colorado River.

A couple of miles to the Eagle River, and we were back to civilization. I was quickly reminded of the real world as I pulled out onto Interstate 70 amid the drone of eighteen-wheelers and morning commuters. Cars were flying by us, going both directions. "God, check out the looks on those faces," I told the dogs. "They are all frantically fighting for first place in line...so anxious, so intense...kinda sad, isn't it?

"It makes you wonder if they even realize they are driving on one of the most incredible highway construction accomplishments of the twentieth century. It took them over ten years and I don't know how many hundreds of millions of dollars to carve a bed for I-70 out of the granite walls of Glenwood Canyon." The pups were giving up on me. They were turning around and around on the seat—it was nap time.

"Oh, no you don't," I said. "Sit up here. I've got a story to tell you about your great-grandfather, Web. Just looking into the eyes of those commuters takes me back to a time when Web and I were doing demonstrations for a big outdoor trade show in the city.

"Because I wasn't accustomed to parking in the big city, I ended up several blocks from the convention center where the show was being held. Oh, I saw some parking spaces closer, but while I was trying to be polite and accommodating to the other drivers, they screeched and jerked into the vacancies like their lives depended on it. Even after I let them park in front of me, they jumped from their cars and glared at me, as if to say, 'Do you want to make something of it?'

"I was clearly out of my element, but what the heck. I love to walk, four or five blocks is no big deal. I paid the parking attendant half a month's rent and Web and I started walking toward the convention center. I hate the smell of the city. I was already getting a dull headache. I could only imagine how it was affecting Web.

"People were streaming by us on both sides, just like these drivers here in the canyon...only lots more of them. They were blank-faced and worried about whatever they were staring at. It must be some magnetic power or something, they all looked straight ahead without so much as a glance to either side.

" 'Mornin', ' " I offered, as one delightful looking young lady passed by. 'Huh. She must not have heard me. Howdy, Mister, how's it going? I guess that guy must have been in a hurry, Web.'

"Finally I stopped in the middle of the sidewalk and Web sat down beside me. We just stood our ground while the wave of people parted to either side of us until they went past, and then merged back in together. Web was looking back and forth and I was leaning backward, trying to see to the top of the office buildings. 'Not much sunshine in here, Web, no wonder all these people are so uptight, it's like they're living in a cave. They sure dress nice, though.

I've never seen so many suits and ties.'

"All of the sudden, I heard a cracklin' voice holler out, 'Hey, nice dog, man.' 'Where do you think that's coming from?' I asked Web.

" 'Hey, that's a damn nice dog you got there, buddy.' I heard it again. This time I matched the voice with the man. He was sitting next to a bus stop bench, on a little snatch of littered grass. He was a grizzled old vagrant who was obviously wearing everything he owned. His broad smile revealed a yellow scum coating on what remained of his teeth. His hair was knotted and greasy. He was wearing a dirty baseball cap with the logo patch torn off.

"I turned and slid through the crowd and pulled up on the bench. 'Yeah,' I said, 'He is a nice dog. His name is Web.' He put his arm around Web's neck and started to play wrestle with him. I watched as he and Web rolled around together. The man's eyes were soft and loving. No matter what conditions had brought him to his present state, it sure as hell wasn't a mean temper or an ornery spirit.

"I sat and observed what I could see of a day in the city until the bum touched me on the shoulder. 'Damon's my name, what's yours?' His grimy hand was stuck out to me, and I grabbed it.

" 'Mike Gould,' I answered as we shook hands. He reached behind the bench and drug out a wrinkled-up brown paper bag wrapped around a bottle of some kind.

" 'I like to have a drink with my friends,' Damon said.

" 'Iiiit's still a little early for me, but I'll have a sip to your friendship, too,' I said. Without being too obvious, I wiped the bottle off the best I could with my shirtsleeve. It took everything I had to take a drink out of that bottle, but I'm glad I did. It was some kind of wine, I think. Ol' Damon laughed and took a deep pull for himself.

"I reached down and took hold of Web's lead and stood to leave. 'Take care of yourself, Damon, I'm glad we met,' I said. I could hear him laugh as Web and I walked away. 'Me, too, Mike, me too,' he said. I looked down at Web as he questioned the obvious. 'I'm afraid to guess what I just drank, Web, but the company out here on the sidewalk would surely sooner kill me than ol' Damon's private stock.' "

The pups had long since tired of my story and dropped off to sleep, so I was pretty much telling it to myself. I hoped they had absorbed the meaning of the story. A guy shouldn't go through life staring straight ahead, ignoring his fellow man, oblivious to his surroundings. There is always opportunity for illumination and education. I have forgotten most of what happened at that sport show, but I have a vivid memory of Damon, his grubby lifestyle, and his wonderful smile. Damon represented the lowest of the low, but he was quick to offer his hand in friendship, and he was the only person that day who noticed a magnificent Labrador walking just below eye level.

I gassed up in Glenwood Springs and headed toward Aspen as I prepared myself for some heavy dickering. All that has been held dear for millions of years is being thrown to the winds in what amounts to a modern-day gold rush throughout the Roaring Fork Valley and most of the mountainous region of Colorado.

City dwellers are fleeing the pressing crowds and evolving violence and are seeking peace and solitude in the mountains. Nowadays, a businessman can run his entire business from the porch of his mountain retreat. Big-time developers have sent surveyors scurrying over the countryside like women at an everything's-a-dollar sale. Realtors are drooling all over their steering wheels as they dash from one end of the valley to the other to seek out new development opportunities.

I made sure I was presentable as I pulled into the driveway of my first appointed stop. "Nice place," I muttered to myself as I walked into the decadent entry toward the front door. After ringing the bell three or four times, I decided to look over by the garage. I had an appointment, the guy was supposed to pay me for three months' training. I spotted a young Mexican girl carrying a big basket of laundry from the guest quarters to the main house.

"Say, can I give you a hand with that?" I asked.

"No, sir, I've got it okay, can I help you?" she replied.

"Yes, I'm supposed to meet the owners here today at 10:00

a.m. It's regarding their dog."

"I'm sorry, sir, they have left for Brazil. They won't be back for three weeks."

"Three weeks, huh? Could you check and see if they left me an envelope or anything? My name's Mike Gould; I'd certainly appreciate it."

The girl pushed through a huge wrought-iron gate and disappeared through the side door of the mansion. "Must be the servant's entrance," I gritted to myself. I knew she wouldn't find anything. I knew they hadn't left me any money. I'd been through this act so many times, I never really expected it.

I wasn't dead yet. I still had two other chances to hit paydirt today. I had to be in Aspen shortly, so I whipped it out onto the highway and sped toward Sin City.

They say some of the finest restaurants in the world are in Aspen, and I was supposed to meet my party at one of them. I slowed down and turned into the private drive of the restaurant. Several young men wearing white sports jackets, black ties and slacks came out of nowhere, and one of them yanked my door open. "Good afternoon, sir," he cheerfully greeted. "May I park you car, sir?"

"I guess so," I said. "Will you please put it in the shade? I've got two pups in here."

"Sure thing," he politely responded, as he left me standing on the brick driveway.

Two of the valets came up to me and told me I was expected. They asked me to follow them into the building. They were smiling. Come to think of it, everyone was smiling. "I'm supposed to be meeting someone here..." I began.

"We know, Mr. Gould. Right this way, sir. You will dine in private quarters. Did you know our chef is one of the finest in the world?"

"Yeah, I've heard something about it. This place is pretty impressive, for sure."

My escort led me into a small dining room where I saw my appointment waiting for me. The waiter turned to me and said, "Your party, sir...my name's Keith, if there's anything you need while you're here, please don't hesitate to call on me."

"Thanks, Keith, I appreciate it, you're doing a heck of a job here," I said.

I walked over to the table and greeted one of my regular clients, a pair of realtors, and the land developer. We were friendly, chatting about birds, dogs, and natural resources while servers fairly swarmed us like we were something special. The famous chef came to our table and presented us with one of his trademark appetizers.

I was maneuvering my way through lunch when the developer spoke up. "I want you to set up your wildlife program on a piece of land I own downvalley," he said. "You come highly recommended. Your reputation is very good."

"Thank you, sir," I said. "Which ranch are you referring to?"

"Are you familiar with the lower valley?" he asked.

"Yes, sir. I'm a local kid. I have a pretty decent feel for all of the ranches in this country. I've run bird dogs on many of them and have released game birds on some. Are you planning on a long-term project?"

"No," he said. "The land will be developed into approximately fifty building lots and a top-end sporting facility and golf complex."

"When will that take place?" I asked.

"It will start sometime next year, but you could live on the place free until then," he offered. "You can run your complete program if you want to. We would love to have you. The deal's on the table."

"Well, it was sure nice meeting you folks, and I truly enjoyed the lunch, but I don't think there is anything for me there," I said. "My eyes cloud up just driving past all these golf courses. Have any of you thought of a project that would showcase the remarkable natural resources that actually brought all of you to this area? Has anyone put the pencil on ranching for wildlife and commercial resource management?

"I have a program within me that can generate several million dollars every year without building so much as one house. You can enjoy a viable, money-making business without compromising the integrity of the natural resources. The end result is an unbelievable enhancement of your holdings, and a permanent, positive solution to some complex land use issues.

"Nothing worthwhile can be accomplished by setting up on your land until the dozers push me into the river. I realize the valley is too far gone to consider this kind of project, but I just wish one person would look at the value of it. Once the houses are all built, and private golf facilities are constructed, the future of the valley is cast. There is no going back. It's a goddamned shame."

The developer squirmed a little but came back strong. "My investors have entrusted me to control and manage all of their property to the highest and best use possible. We now own nearly all of the prime development land from Glenwood Springs on up.

"I can assure you, I intend to safeguard all of the resources to the best of my ability. Our master plan has addressed all of the pertinent natural values. We have employed the best professionals available to attend to every detail of local and regional concern. We own that property outright, we control it, and before it's over we're going to make a pile of money off of it."

The structure of the meeting was now very apparent to me. My client was a well-connected old friend who was just trying to help me out. The two realtors were acting as support for the developer. It's like you see in the movies...the crime boss always has his muscle lying in the wings, just in case there's trouble.

I looked at the realtors. They were sitting side by side with the same condescending look on their faces. It was like a cosmetic smirk, an uppity implant. The developer was still talking to me, but I was thinking to myself how the realtors might have gone to the same plastic surgeon. I could see it now. The doctor asks, "What look are you seeking here?"

The realtor answers, "One of superiority, one of wisdom... one of wealth."

The ol' doctor nods and responds, "Yeah, that's what everybody wants; how do you plan to pay, cash or credit card?"

I turned back to the developer and patiently listened to the remainder of his spiel. I knew it would be my turn then. I knew the meeting was a bust and I knew nothing I was about to say would make a bit of difference to them—but it did to me.

"Sir, you asked me if I was familiar with the ranches you were referring to," I began. "The answer is yes. I lived on one of them back in the sixties, and I lived on another for six years from 1988 to 1993.

"I want to begin by saying, I'm not a professional. I do not have a degree in anything. I'm a dog trainer, an observer of life, and a chronic dreamer. I do have some questions for you, and some comments that you may or may not find helpful.

"I can't help but wonder how this master plan of yours works. For example: how many eagles do you plan to summon to your cottonwoods in January, and how many great blue herons will come later in the spring? How many times each year will you cause the clouds to grow dark over your property, and how many days will you allow the sun to shine? How many raindrops do you figure will be enough to nourish this land of yours? How much snow cover have your professionals allotted to protect your seedlings from the cold? Have you decided how high the river should be, and are there applied principles to keep it within its banks?

"Will you still let stonefly nymphs crawl out to hatch on your willows? What will you do when your fifty homeowners and your golfing guests complain about the caddis flies that come off the river every Mother's Day? They are beyond number. Many times it seems as though it is snowing from the ground up.

"Do I know about these ranches? Not as much as I'd like to. I have personally touched many of the rocks throughout the riverbottom. Hundreds of days I've walked the fields and admired the unusual mix of tansy and reed canary grass that grows along the ditches.

"I was deeply saddened when I realized a boring beetle was taking the last few remaining ponderosa pines from the bottoms. I guess you knew, either the Colorado Midland or the old Elkhorn Railroad used that area to switch engines and turn around. As you excavate, you might keep an eye out for railway or Indian artifacts.

"The original settlement of the valley was a Ute Indian village known as Sutank that just happened to be located directly across the river from your place. My grandfather's brother married the first white child born in that village.

"I loved the storied old box elder tree near the river house. I hope your plans are to preserve it. I have seen a hundred mountain bluebirds in one day there, I have watched avocet stalk your ponds, and osprey sweep great brown trout into the air.

"I have laid out in your fields for hours until I was sure I could feel the heartbeat. You know they were formed in alluvium, don't you? You know that each handful of soil was brought to your land from virtually every mountain around it...don't you?

"You must certainly know there are at least seven natural springs that course through the veins of the gravelly substratum beneath your topsoil. I will share with you—one of those springs has a precocious sense of humor. It seems as though there is quite a bit of gypsum within your subsoil. It lies in big pockets. Gypsum dissolves like sugar when it gets wet, and every now and then a big sinkhole will show up out in those fields. You surely knew the history of those sinkholes, didn't you? A sudden sinkhole in the ninth fairway is really no big deal, but let that happen in the living room of a five-million-dollar house. That'll have the lawyers going for their guns.

"The real truth, to my way of thinking, is this: you don't own that land, sir. You never will. You are only a temporary steward. All mother earth has to do is shrug her shoulders, and your effort will next be recorded by archaeologists and geologists. Entire civilizations have been lost in the blink of an eye, and usually the world was better off for it. You have a choice. You can either care for the land you are presently responsible for, or you can go ahead with your development plans. I have no doubt which way you'll go."

I was out of gas. I breathed deep and took a drink of water. Everyone else was looking at the table. No one said a word, so I stood up.

"Yes, sir, I know a little about your ranches," I continued. "I know I love them beyond words. I am extremely grateful for having the chance to spend the time I did there. When developers forced me off the first time, it broke my heart. I'm not sure if I will ever recover completely. I do appreciate your having asked me here, and I wish you the best of luck with your project. I've got two pups chewing on my gear shift knob right now, and I'm a little over two hours from camp. If I can get ol' Keith to come up with my truck, I'll be heading on home. I don't even know why I go to these meetings. I don't know why I put myself through the grief. Sooner or later I'll have to face the fact—the valley's lost, bought and sold, come and gone."

I thanked them again for lunch and followed Keith out to my truck. "I'd love to tip you, Keith," I explained, "but I'm afraid I can't get 'er done today."

Okay, it was time to get serious. I still hadn't raked in a dime, and my possibilities were growing slim. I reminded myself to stay loose, to stay in there. All of the sudden opportunity presented itself. Lo and behold, I saw a training client that had owed me money for six months. He was casually walking with some friends.

I drove by where he couldn't miss seeing me, while I pretended not to notice him. I was actually baiting him. If he felt the urge to pay me some money, he would stop me. If he didn't, he would act like he hadn't made me. This type approach would save me time and effort. If he gave me the cold shoulder, there wasn't much sense in pulling over and hitting him up for the dough. Chances are he wouldn't come through.

It worked!

"Hey, Mike! Mike...hey, Gould, hey, hey," he hollered. I was grinning to myself as I pulled over to the side of the road. "Ching," I said out loud to the dogs, "it's payday."

"Bet you thought I forgot about you," he joked as he hustled up to my truck. He looked at the dogs. "Hey, who you got in there with you?"

"Oh, just a couple of my pups," I said casually. "I'm hoping to get them into some birds on the way back to camp. How are you getting along with your dog these days?"

"Good lookin' pups," he enthused. "My dog's doing a dandy job for me. We're heading out to the opening of pheasant in South Dakota next month. Say, while I'm thinking of it, I would like to pay you some on my training bill. If I had my checkbook with me, I would pay it all, but I'm sure I've got some change here."

He dug around in his pocket and came out with a silver money clip that was poked full of bills. "If you wouldn't put so much money in that thing, it wouldn't get so stretched out," I teased.

"Yeah, you caught me at a pretty good time," he said. "I can spare a couple hundred bucks for you."

I hate it when I talk to clients in front of their friends. They always act like they are doing me such a great favor, like it's some kind of magnanimous gesture or something. Nevertheless, I appreciated the money, and I damn sure needed it. I didn't even have enough gas to make it back to camp, much less go anywhere once I got there.

"You can mail the rest if you want to," I offered. "I'm certainly glad your dog is doing well. Please let me know if I can help in any way."

Me and the dogs broke out of there before the sky started falling. "Let's get to the house," I said. "You guys stay low and I'll act regular until we're in the clear."

We tore out of town like we had just robbed the bank. We were lucky—we had run into someone who owed me money. The trick was to get out of there before we ran into someone I owed money to.

I stopped in Glenwood, filled the ol' gas tank to the brim, snagged a six-pack of beer and a few camp supplies. I knew once I felt the walls of the canyon closing about me, I was pretty much back on the beam. I turned up the radio and tapped on the steering wheel.

Without a doubt, the last two hours of daylight is my favorite time of day. It's a magical time. The animals feel a need to catch a little supper, and the sun lays out flat to change the harsh light of midday into a soul-softening glow. This is photographer's light—it draws from the day the deepest and richest color, and lays it thick across the countryside.

As I climbed out of the canyon, I cast a longing gaze into the dark shadows of the hillside while I cranked around each switchback. On right-hand corners, I would ease out onto the edge of the wrong side of the road and splash one searching eye out into the oak brush, while the other tested the road ahead for the dust of a logging truck. It's frightful enough to meet one of those timber-haulers when you're taking up your half, but they'll stop your heart when they come upon you dangling off of their side.

I stopped long enough to count points on a couple of dandy little mule deer bucks and faithfully noted the whistle pigs, squirrels and rabbits who had honed their personal survival skills along the edges of the road. At the very top, there stood two weathered sentries. They are a pair of nearly identical limber pines who had been standing dead as long as I could remember. They had withstood unbelievable circumstances while they dutifully guarded the interests of their brotherhood. I call them "Los Pinos Bravo."

We were just coming into a little park of mostly stunted sagebrush when I saw a hen blue grouse dusting just off the right side of the road. I drove by like I didn't see her and pulled over a hundred yards up the road.

"You kids have been putting up with me and my deals all day. Now it's time for you to start earning your keep. Let's see what we can dig out of that sagebrush back there," I told them.

If you see a hen grouse that time of year, it usually means a covey. I swung the pups out into the park to let them loosen up before we inquired of the wind, "Can you tell us of your treasure?" I stood and watched as the soft evening wind whispered her secrets into the glistening noses of my pups. These were secrets they would never forget; these were secrets they would teach their children. I crunched a dried gentian head in my glove while they careened from bush to bush until their promise was fulfilled.

The hen was still there, along with seven of her finest. She clucked them into a nearby quakie thicket, where they peered down at the dogs as they mobbed the sagebrush and dashed back and forth from the trees to the park.

They ran up to me and bounced up on my waist. "Pay the man!" they urged. "Can we go again, did you see that, can we go again, there were twenty at least, maybe fifty, can we go again?"

I walked over to the truck and poured some water into a dish. "Yeah, you can go again," I said, "but I'm afraid you wore that covey plumb out. If you sit up and pay attention, maybe we'll get to boost another before we get to camp."

The setting sun and reflections of the day kept my mind busy while I cruised past the spring and turned up the hill towards camp. Grizzly Creek was in the dark already, and I wanted to get to camp to help Danny with the evening chores.

I was admiring the alders of Broken Rib Bottoms when I caught a slight movement to my left. Instinctively, I quickly stopped and there they were, the same six bulls. I turned the truck off. This time they were within forty yards of me, broadside. "Well, I'll be damned," I said. "They haven't moved since this morning." The dogs crowded into my lap to see for themselves. The elk were close, and they were gorgeous. The evening sun had them all singled out and lit up like they were plastic. This was one of those times when you can breathe the essence of life. We stared at each other—six elk, two dogs, and me. They fed up into a small patch of Douglas fir and I again started up the hill.

A few minutes later, we bumped into camp to see Danny going about his chores. I jumped out and pitched in. After we got the dogs in order, Danny whipped up a fire and I rustled the coffeepot. "Just in time for supper," Danny said.

"What we havin'?" I asked.

"Nostaws Crispy Burrito Express," Danny replied.

"Are we using the fixins from last night?" I laughed.

"Darned right," Danny said. "You know it's always better on the second day. I'm gonna add some jalapenos and a few spuds. It should be dynamite."

Before long we were folding tortillas around Danny's famous Epicurean delight. Little beads of sweat popped out on my forehead with the first bite, and reminded me I had some beer sitting in ice over at the truck. Danny laughed as I sprinted to fetch us some relief.

"How'd the dogs do today?" I asked.

"I had a great day," he said. "I got everybody worked and took a long walk out to the rim." Danny went on to tell me about his day of training and what he worked on with each dog. Halfway through he paused to tell me a small thunderstorm had passed through early that afternoon. I told him about seeing the elk and the covey of grouse. I dug in my pocket and came up with half the money I'd picked up and gave it to him. I told him the other guy wouldn't be paying for at least three weeks.

We were poking the fire with our own favorite sticks while the dogs settled in for the night. "Looks like there's one more beer each, Danny," I said as I gimped to my feet and made my way to the cooler.

"How'd the rest of the day go?" Danny asked.

"Oh, about the usual. We won some and we lost some."

"I don't know about you, Mike, but I'm bushed," he said. "I think I'm going to hit it. Pretty nice bulls, huh?" Danny walked over and hopped up on the dog box and started dragging his boots off.

I decided to sit for a minute before I put the fire out. "Yeah, they sure were. Oh yeah, I brought you some more Coleman fuel, there, Firemaster.

"Say, Danny..."

He was wrestling with the zipper on his sleeping bag as he replied, "What's that, Mike?"

"I was just wondering...what do you think the poor people are doing tonight?"

We both laughed.

The day is quickly coming, my friend,
I'll release you from your tether.
Forevermore we'll depend upon
The bond we share together.

Over and Behind 'Em

Guiding bird hunters is much like being a bartender. Hundreds of shooters come into your life for one day, and for one reason. Like the bartender, a hunting guide learns the trick nature of reading the clientele and avoiding problems by anticipation and subtle adjustments in style. Some need encouragement, some need instruction, some need a helping hand, others a firm one.

The trouble generally will come from the head, or leader, of the group. This person is almost always a man, and many times he is the boss. He is used to hiring and firing, making decisions—making things happen.

If he is in charge of arranging the hunt, or paying for it, he is usually reeling from self-imposed pressure to produce. When the guide first meets the group, this stressed-out commander will push to the front and take center stage.

I developed early on the ability to memorize each of the shooters' first names as we shook hands at introduction. I liked to spend a few minutes talking about the hunt and what we were about to do. I would tell them about the dogs we would be hunting over and I would inquire about the guns and loads they were using. Naturally, I always asked if anyone was an experienced wingshooter, and if others needed assistance. Then we'd talk about gun safety as I tactfully pointed out the necessity.

All of the things we were talking about were important, for sure, but the real reason I needed this time with the shooters was to seek out what potential problems I saw, and identify who I considered to be the bad apple.

They way they stood, the way they dressed, their gun-handling habits, and their overall attitude gave me all the information I needed to make things go smoothly for them.

You can always tell how much bird hunting a fellow has done by the way he talks on the way out in the morning. Experienced scattergunners stay pretty quiet about the time the newcomer starts telling of his shooting prowess. They secretly know the poor guy is digging a hole, and if he keeps at it, he'll set himself up for certain trouble when the birds start coming up.

I remember one hunt I did for a group of state wildlife officials. Just the idea of guiding men who considered themselves to be a grade above the common man made me cringe a little. State wildlife officers are not accustomed to being shown where the wildlife actually is. They fancy themselves the ultimate warrior, even though most of them spend their workdays behind a desk.

I was to meet my hunters at 4:00 a.m. on the second Monday of grouse season. We planned to hook up at the 7-11 parking lot in Glenwood Springs, Colorado. They wanted to discuss some business during the hunt, so they brought their own rig and planned to follow along behind me.

I had been scouting for grouse for six solid weeks prior, and had the birds pretty well pegged. This hunt was just as important to me as it was to my guests. I had been preaching from a soapbox for many years to the deaf ear of the state wildlife bureaucracy. I wanted to plead my case in the field before men who could make a change, that they should take their grouse seriously, they should plan to take care of them like they do the fish and the other game animals.

Even though they didn't deserve it, I saved the honey hole for them. If it's grouse they came to see, they wouldn't forget this day.

I had been running grouse hunts for about ten days already, so I felt pretty confident as I pulled into the parking lot. I swung my lights across some vehicles in the lot, and then stopped under the street light. I jumped out to grab some coffee, thinking they must not be here yet. Wup...back up, there they are, over there by themselves. Okay, let's see, a brand-new four-wheel-drive with about five thousand dollars' worth of gear piled in the back—that's them for sure.

I walked over, introduced myself and shook some hands. "You guys ready?" I asked. "Do you need to get some coffee or anything?"

"Nope, we're all set here."

"Sounds good, I'll be out in a second. You can follow me."

I was trying to figure out how to drink out of that little slit in the plastic lid as I walked back across the parking lot. I saw a big happy-faced guy looking into the rear section of his vehicle, busily arranging the gear.

"I brought two guns today," he hollered. "I've been shooting a lot of sporting clay tournaments lately, and couldn't decide which one would do the best job."

"I don't think it will matter much which gun you shoot," I replied, "but I hope you brought plenty of shells. It looks like it's going to be pretty windy out there today."

"Oh, I brought plenty of shells, all right," he laughed. "These guys I'm with couldn't hit your hat if you threw it up. I'll probably have to shoot their limits, too."

"Kind of an odd statement, coming from a game warden," I thought to myself as I hopped back into my truck and fired it up. Oh, well, I knew he was in for a tough day. He might of got by with the talk of two guns and all the sporting clay tournaments, but his claim to help his friends with their limits would surely be his downfall.

That day we were hunting on an absolute myriad of ridges and draws known as the Roan Plateau. Most of the ridges top out at about 8,000 feet, so we're pretty much talking about the sub-alpine terrain and habitat. They go on for miles, most with a partially beaten two-track road that splits the ridge into fairly even halves.

I had saved a special ridge for this group, partly because I knew it held at least 70 grouse along the top, and partly because it was very easy walking.

I tended to the dogs that I wouldn't be using for the first hour or two, and loaded them back into their kennels to relax. I released two Labs in front of three shooters and headed down the ridge, cross-wind. Handling two dogs on these ridge tops takes a lot of concentration, especially along the sloping shoulders of the ridge.

I was working over at one side when I heard the big happy-faced guy start shooting. The shots came in sets of two... four of them.

"Wow, eight shots. He must have waded into a big covey," I said to myself. I was hustling through the brush so I could help pick up birds and find out what was happening.

When I got there, he was turning around and around in a big clump of sagebrush. He was actually stumbling as he turned, because he was still looking skyward. His gun was held at port arms and the look on his face was hard to describe. It was like Publishers' Clearing House had just stopped by to inform him he had won ten million dollars, but he wasn't home, so they gave it to his neighbor.

He finally quit turning and stood still. "How many did you get?" I asked.

"None!" he barked. He was still staring out into the distance at about shoulder level.

"None?" I queried.

"Yep, none," came the retort.

"Did you watch the covey down?" I asked. "You might have rattled one or two."

"No, I missed 'em clean, I'm sure of that," he said. "I don't have any idea where they went. I don't know where I was shooting."

"You were over and behind 'em," I said, as I sent the dogs on.

"What did you say?"

"I said you were over and behind 'em. Remember to keep your head down and swing through."

The big happy-faced guy let his arms go slack and jolt to his sides. He turned to me and glared like a serial killer. "How the hell do you know where I was shooting?" he demanded. "You weren't even over here!"

"Easy," I said. "I've been around hundreds of wing shooters and I know birds. I know I wasn't here when they went—but I do know approximately where they went, and how they got there.

"Grouse fly like partridge in this country. They flush into the wind and then break off the top in a downward, curving pattern. They left your shot-string about a foot high, and at least two feet behind them.

"You were over because it's hard to keep your head down on a target while it's cutting down and away. You were behind because nobody shoots in front of a grouse, and besides, it's unnatural to swing through in a downward motion.

"Oh, by the way, do you want to pick up some of these shells? Some of them are still good. Boy! Eight in the air and five on the ground. At this rate, you're gonna run out of ammo for sure."

I heard the guy mutter to himself as he struck out to catch up with the others. "I'll change to stiffer loads," he mumbled. "That'll do it. I'm gonna try my rose-colored glasses. I just couldn't see those birds."

I shouldn't have said anything to him, but I just couldn't resist. I normally don't try to help shooters unless they ask for it, but this guy had it coming. Oh, well, he didn't pay any attention, anyway, I thought.

Throughout the morning we were able to find kinder coveys that enabled him to climb back on his high horse.

The dogs rested as we camped for lunch. This stop is critical, because this is where I get a chance to size the hunters up as far as the afternoon hunt is concerned. I like to take a fairly long lunch break, mainly because we start so early.

One of the dogs had split a pad, so I jumped him up on the tailgate to put a boot on his foot. These guys were turning out to be a likeable lot, and I was feeling pretty good with the hunt overall. I was fumbling through my first aid kit when I heard the big guy talk about his shooting. I couldn't believe he had brought it up again, so I turned my back and pretended not to hear what he had to say.

I couldn't ignore him any longer, as he included me in the

conversation by hollering in my direction. "Hey, Mike, what was all that jazz you were giving me about being over and behind those birds?"

"What are you talking about?" one of his friends asked.

"Oh, Mike was trying to tell me where I was shooting without even watching me."

"Happens the same way with pheasant, too," I commented without turning around.

"Well, pheasant sure as hell don't fly like these birds," he snorted. "I don't understand what you mean."

I was cornered. I tossed my tape into the first aid kit and walked over to join in. "It happens on pheasant for a different reason," I explained. "With grouse, it's the downward curve of their flight that causes a shooter to shoot over and behind them. With pheasant, it's the shape of the bird. Let me try to explain.

"Pheasants are very streamlined birds that come to a point at the tip of their long tail feathers. Just the sheer beauty of a rooster pheasant alone has caused many shooters to lift their heads just before they pull the trigger. It is very easy to let your eyes slip along the smooth lines of a pheasant, and without even knowing it, you may end up shooting at his tail. Even if you swing through dramatically, you probably will never catch up to him. A person has to teach himself to shoot at the ring, just behind the bird's head, then swing through smoothly while keeping his head down on the gunstock.

"Many geese are missed, and many more are wounded and never recovered, because of a similar problem. When you first see a goose come into shooting range, your eye is automatically drawn to that big chest. The goose's chest is layered with thick, armor-like feathers that can absorb a pretty substantial load. The bones of the inner wing, namely the humerus, radius, and the ulna, are the strongest in the bird's body. You may be shooting at the area of the bird that has the most protection. If a guy fights off the urge to look at the chest, and then moves out to the head—well, geese are easy pickin's when they are in range.

"I've noticed every game bird species has its own unique method of tricking shooters. Some covey birds are accomplished at mass confusion, while others rely on optical illusion.

"The same rules hold true in those sporting clays tournaments you're competing in. Stand behind shooters while they're in the cage, and a high percentage of the misses are over and behind. When things are going bad for me out there, I just remind myself to relax, keep my head down, and keep swinging."

Now these guys are businessmen, they are used to telephones, fax machines, computers, crowds, traffic and schedules. They had just finished lunch, and, for the first time that day, they were starting to relax. They were a little more tired than they thought.

Gratefully, an adult goshawk changed the topic of conversation as he came out of nowhere and cruised down the ridge. "That bird was mighty quick," on of the hunters chipped in. "I could see his muscles rippling from under his chest feathers."

A mellowness settled in amidst my guests. We started talking about the neighboring mountains and the oil shale projects that were cropping up all over the Colorado Northwest. We discussed the valleys and the shortage of water that fall.

Just think of it—we had been out there for over six hours, and finally they had settled down enough to enjoy the resources that they were entrusted to safeguard. Limits of birds were no longer all that important. Everyone was quiet as we drove slowly to another ridge. We were all looking for elk, looking for deer, watching for coyote sign or a grouse dusting in the road. "Now we're getting somewhere," I thought to myself.

This is the time in a hunt where an experienced guide starts to unplug the hunters. They are all tired, but of course no one wants to be the first to bring it up. The second best time of day to hunt grouse is right at dusk, so I decided to work a few small ridges on our way out.

During the afternoon, our minds were full of our own personal thoughts, and our eyes were now getting sore from straining to the skyline and beyond. Now, as darkness came calling, each man became truly reflective and soft. They shifted their weight occasionally to relieve a particular sore spot, only to be reminded that it was the whole body that was hurting. Men are funny about feeling this way. They complain about their discomfort, but they love it nonetheless. It's like working very hard and feeling so good about being tired afterward.

Our vision was confined to the headlights as the highway stretched out like a carpet toward home. After driving mountain roads all day, the pavement really did feel like soft carpet.

I didn't hear a peep out of the dog boxes. They were tired, too. I wondered if they were all okay. I usually like to check them thoroughly before I put them to bed, because the next day was to be another work day for them and for me. My dogs were professional athletes, just like ball players. They have to play hurt sometimes, sometimes they have to step up when they really don't feel like it. They know I'll be depending on them, and they'll be ready.

I pulled into the 7-11 parking lot. I got out and walked over to their vehicle, while they were crawling out and groaning in unison. They were all smiles behind dirt and sunburn.

"Sure seems like we've been gone longer than one day," I said.

"Not long enough," one hunter replied. "I think we should do this every year."

"I appreciate that," I said. "It sounds good to me." Ol' Happy-face reached out and shook my hand. "Thanks for a great day," he said. As he turned away, he left three hundred-dollar bills in my palm. They all piled back in and started for home.

"I'll bet that's the only time that rig will ever be in four-wheel-drive," I thought to myself. They were good folks, though. I had a good day with them. I noticed their brake lights come on just before they pulled out of the parking lot. They started backing up toward me. As they stopped, the big happy-faced guy poked his head out of the driver's window.

"Thanks again," he laughed, "and remember…when things are going rough for you out there, you're over and behind 'em. Keep your head down and swing through."

I couldn't stop grinning as I crawled into my truck. "Oh, well," I thought, "I've got some chores to do…and damn, I'm feeling a little creaky myself."

A bird dog not only smells the bird, he tastes it as well.
He senses the presence of his fulfillment, even before he sees it.

He stands there on faith alone.
When everything within him says to move, make something happen,
he's decided to simply let something happen.
How could he have achieved this wisdom
before his third birthday.

The Fire Truck Story

What do you want to be when you grow up?

Kids are asked that one unbelievable question every day of every year. Surprisingly enough, many of them already have an idea as to what they would like to become.

I don't know if anyone ever drug me off my stick horses to ask me such an important question. I know I wouldn't have answered with any of the standard responses, like "policeman," "fireman," "the President of the United States," "the richest man on earth," or "the greatest scientist of all time."

I would've liked to become the best shot in town. That would have come in handy, but it wouldn't have paid much. I knew for a fact that I didn't want to buck hay bales or pick spuds for a living. Herding cows never made any sense, and it still doesn't.

Getting elected to a government position wasn't much of a challenge. All you had to do was ride around on floats in parades with your belly poking out like you were something special. You had to practice until you could lie convincingly and look down on someone else...even though it might be your mom, or your cousin.

Being a banker never really appealed to me. Most folks around my hometown dreaded going into the bank as much as they did the dentist's office. I just instinctively knew the men who came out of

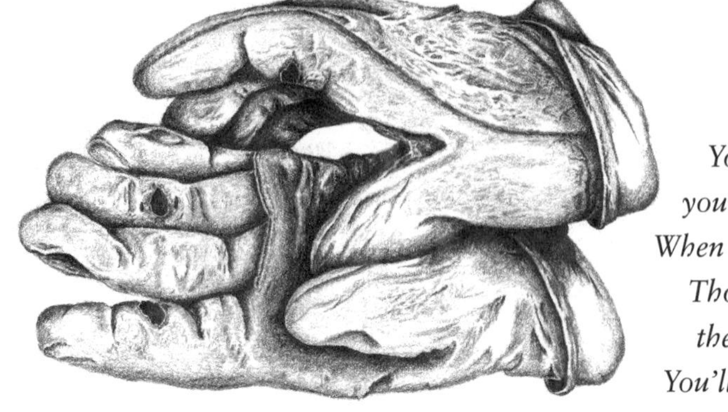

Your gloves are as
your loves, you know,
When life spins you about.
Though try you may,
there's just one way
You'll ever wear 'em out.

the bank with their knees all scraped up and bleeding hadn't just fallen down while they were depositing a bag full of money. Besides that, the banker was another one who always had that pasted-on smile, and a belly big enough to dance on.

The real truth is, I don't trust anyone who doesn't wear gloves. You see, if you're wearing gloves, chances are you're planning on doing some work. Gloves are a good measure of a man. There's only one way to wear 'em out. If there was only one thing I could look at before I threw in with an outfit, I would want to see the boss's gloves.

If I had wanted to be a policeman, I would have had to move. There was already a cop in our town. Outside of a bar fight, or an occasional car wreck, he spent most of his time driving around, looking for the kids who were constantly bouncing apples off his cruiser. I didn't know it at the time, but those apple wars, along with my first real job, prepared me for greater things to come.

Our town was divided roughly into two sections...the south side of Main Street, and the north side of Main Street. I lived on the north, next to the railroad tracks. Raiding gardens and harassing the cop were about the only things to do until kids got old enough to drive. It turns out there were special skills required of one that paid off big time while doing the other.

For instance, in order to do a decent job of raidin' a garden, you have to stake out the place and do some surveillance work. It helped if you had a lawn mowin' job. You could make a few bucks while you checked out most of the gardens in town. Also you could gain valuable information as to whose apples were ready and whose weren't. You had a good reason for walking around in back of everyone's houses—you were simply mowing and clipping.

While some of my friends went the lawn mowin' route, I didn't like it. Oh, I mowed some of the lawns in my immediate neighborhood, but after all, I knew all I needed to know about those places. I would generally try to con my sisters into doing all the work, especially the clipping. God, I hated that.

I decided a newspaper route was the best way to go for me. I ended up with 33 houses on my route. I delivered the *Daily Sentinel*—it was a seven-day-a-week job.

I thought about being a newspaperman when I grew up, but when I took into consideration that they have to work through hunting season, that left me out. There was one miscalculation I made regarding the newspaper business: it was way too steady. While my lawn mowin', bale buckin', spud pickin' buddies were laying around all winter, I still had to deliver the newspaper seven days a week.

I picked up the papers after school and usually took off on my route around five o'clock in the evening. In the wintertime it usually gets cold right in there somewhere, and dark soon after. I remember one night in particular, I was carrying a thermometer in my coat pocket that was reading 28 below. It was so cold, you could spit on the ground and it would break when it hit.

I think I would've stuck with my paper route if the street to the last ten or twelve houses had had a street light. After I crossed the railroad tracks, I was on my own. It was darker than the inside of a cow down there, and what made matters worse, the town's cemetery was at the end of that road. My family actually owned the cemetery, but I never got any comfort or satisfaction from knowing that. After my sisters flat refused to take over my paper route on a regular basis, I quit the first real job I'd ever had.

I know I said I didn't want to be a fireman, but that isn't the whole truth. The real reason I didn't want to be a fireman was because the mayor told me I couldn't. I personally think I would have made a pretty darn good fireman, and that's why I want to tell you the fire truck story.

One day my dad and I were sitting on the top of a fence, watching the rodeo. The rodeo was part of our town's biggest annual celebration, Potato Day. The whole town was there every year.

Potato Day was great. There was a parade of floats and politicians, the school band, and lots of horses. Some of the town's upper crust would barbecue beef in an underground pit over green oak coals for a whole day or two prior, and all the women from miles around got together and baked spuds. The barbecue lunch was free, and the Potato Day Rodeo followed directly afterward.

The rodeo grounds were located up by the high school, just at the southern edge of town. It was easy walking distance no matter where you started from, so the streets were full of people walking both ways.

There were all the usual rodeo events like buckin' horses and bulls, ropin', and barrel racin'. The winners would barely win enough to pay their doctor bill, but everyone always loved the whole affair. There was one event that promised a big payoff if you won—the Greased Pig Race.

This race was just for kids and you got to keep the pig if you caught it. That made sense to me. I entered the greased pig contest for a couple of years, but then gave it up. You see, lots of us got close enough to jump on the pig and grab him around the neck, but holdin' on was a whole new ballgame. I would hold on for all I was worth, but I never really got the bugs worked out of my technique. The worst part of the whole deal was when you finally had to let go.

A pig can run pretty fast, so there's lots of draggin' and skiddin' involved. There's no way around it, you're gonna end up in the soft dirt of the rodeo ground on your head. When you finally come up, you get run over by all the rest of the kids in town.

Now, my mom made most of my shirts. I don't know how your mom was while you were growing up, but if you want to put things in perspective, try this. Rub a half a tub of Crisco all down the front of your shirt (like they smear on greased pigs), run as fast as you can, and dive into a pile of dirt mixed with cow manure. There's no detergent on earth that will put a dent in that stain, take it from me. Even if I'd won the pig, I don't think it would've kept me from getting a beating.

Anyway, my dad and I were on top of the fence watching the ropin' when the fire siren went off. My dad baled off the back side of the fence and started runnin' toward the fire house, which was about four blocks away. I didn't know exactly what to do, so I rolled off and started running too.

I'd never seen him run before. I looked over my shoulder and damned near every man in town was running too. Hey, now we're talking, I thought, this is a lot better than a pig race.

We were breathing hard as we came around the corner next to the fire house. The siren was wailin' and several cars and trucks were slidin' to a stop just out front. The doors flew open and everyone jumped into action.

Here's the routine: the first guy to get to the phone takes the message, including where the fire is and who called it in. He then turns and writes the information on a big chalk board right next to the phone, so everyone will know what's going on. Somebody climbs in, starts the truck, and pulls it out of the garage. Usually about four or five men will hop up on the rear of the fire truck, where they will hold onto a big chrome rail and ride to the fire location. When the truck pulls out into the street, all the cars and trucks, who have been waiting outside, fall into line and follow the screaming fire truck to the fire.

That day my dad and I got there just as the truck was comin' out. He jumped up on the back and said, "Come on, kid!" as he extended his hand. Without a second thought I leaped up onto the rear deck and grabbed hold of the rail.

There were some fireman hats and jackets on each side of the truck. My dad wouldn't take off his cowboy hat for love nor money, but he did slip into a long black jacket as we tore down the street and headed out of town. I grabbed a hat and strapped it on. Things were looking up.

I'd been standing in the back of my dad's pickup all my life, so this ride was pretty run-of-the-mill for me, but my heart was pounding. We were going to a fire!

A couple of miles out of town the truck lurched to a stop and everyone started piling out. Some men were grabbing hoses and pulling them out, others were working the pump controls. Everyone was hollering and shouting orders, though I still hadn't seen any flames. One guy dropped a suction hose into Jim Sharp's irrigation ditch and cranked the siphon pump. I was standing over at the side of the road in disbelief. My hat was way too big, so I had it tilted back so I could see. There was no way I was going to take it off. All of a sudden, I saw it. SMOKE!

It was a bad one. A pile of cow manure was on fire and everyone was concerned about it spreading. Some were pounding on the smoldering ground with shovels while others were pouring water everywhere. I saw a shovel, grabbed it, and followed suit.

If you've never put out a manure fire, you shouldn't be too quick to judge the severity of one. They travel underground for a while and then just pop up. You can douse it with water and beat it to a pulp, only to see it resurface ten yards away. After a while we got it put out, got all the equipment stored, and the hoses rolled up. I looked like I'd just crawled out of the coal mine. My eyes were burning and I had blisters on my hands from shoveling. I was just now noticing how tired I was, and it was plain to see that the men were tired also.

More importantly, I was very impressed with the serious attitude the men had taken. Okay, so it was a manure fire. Okay, so nobody's life was in danger. But I learned an important lesson that day: accidental fires are bad, they are all bad and they need to be put out. It's serious business.

I was also impressed with the town's volunteer fire department. Though nobody there was a professional fireman, they were prepared and had all their equipment in place to roll on a moment's notice. This was a smooth operation.

The ride back to town was glorious. I was the only one who rode on the back of the fire truck. I was like a conquering hero returning home from war. I wanted to hold my shovel high as we crossed the railroad tracks and started down Main Street. Now this was a Potato Day. This beat the hell out of dragging behind pigs and shooting peas at politicians.

From then on, no matter where I was, when I heard that fire

siren go off I broke for the station. If it happened during the work week, many of the volunteers would be at work, so the responding firemen were mainly the store owners. My best friend Fergie and I would make every fire we could. We would throw down our baseball mitts if we were at ball practice, and even our fishing poles would go flying when we heard the siren.

We learned right away that the men were cheaters—they could drive. They would jump into their rigs and within a few minutes, they'd pull up in front of the station. Not us. We had to high-foot it from somewhere in town. Like I've said before, the town wasn't much, but it was usually a good stretch to the station.

Sometimes we would skid to a stop at the fire house, only to see the truck disappear at the other end of the street, heading out of town. Clearly we had to change tactics if we were going to stay with our fire-fighting career. Well, that's where all the lawn mowin', paper deliverin', and apple throwin' paid off.

We knew every alley and back yard in town. We knew who had bad dogs and who didn't. We knew the shortest way to the fire house, and we figured it was time to get serious.

Fergie had an advantage over me that I couldn't get around—he was an extremely fast runner. Later on, in high school, he was the state champion sprinter in the 100 and 220 yard dash. I wasn't a fast runner, but I was a good learner. I memorized that town like the inside circuitry of a jukebox. Fergie liked a clean sprint to the finish, while I was perfectly content to jump a ditch and climb a fence or two to get my time down.

Dogs didn't really bother me. Even the biters weren't much of a problem. By the time they realized I was in their yard, their chances of catching me before I hit the back fence were minimal. The trick was, I had to commit to crossing the yard, no matter what. That way I kept my speed entering the yard, and was into the neighbor's place before I knew anybody had been there. Sometimes I would hear a dog hit his fence well after I'd crossed, and occasionally a lady would shake her fist and threaten to call my mom.

Even though I could jump any fence in town, and even though I wasn't worried about the dogs, there were two very real dangers in carrying that kind of speed through people's yards: One, I never knew where they had been watering their lawns, which could make takeoffs and landing perilous; and two, I had to know where the clothesline was, and more importantly, how high it was. Luckily I had worked out all the clothesline details while raiding gardens and stealing apples. Those two activities always took place at night, so I took careful note and never forgot.

My friend, Stony Walsh, was about five inches taller than me. One night he followed me through Mrs. Snyder's back yard at a dead run. I slightly ducked under the clothesline and looked back to see Stony flip into the air and come down on his head. Fergie and I dragged him over by the ditch and hid until he came to. He had a pretty red line across his adam's apple for two weeks. Lucky for him, Mrs. Snyder had plastic clotheslines. One of the wires would have put him down for the count.

Every time we got the chance, we rushed to the siren and helped with the fire. If it was a house fire, we had the good sense to stand back and let the real firemen do their job. If it was a brush fire, or some rancher's haystack, the volunteers were content to stand up on the truck and point as we beat and stomped and drenched everything within reach of our hoses.

On two occasions I made gallant leaping efforts to swing onto the truck long after it had left the station. The first was when Fergie and I were helping my brother Art install a tin roof on a new business in town. We were working on an addition to Berry's Garage. The garage was a full-service gas station and they decided to build a car wash. It sounded crazy to me...I mean, who would pay to wash their own car? That's what you have kids for. Anyway, you just drive in and put a few quarters in this machine...oh, well, it'll never make any money.

Keith Berry owned the garage, and he was also one of the head honchos of the fire department. Fergie and I were up on the roof when the siren sounded. My brother told us to keep working as he and Keith took off in Keith's truck.

We looked at each other, and both jumped off the roof. Fergie was showing his sprinter's form down Main Street while I was hurdling fences and evading dogs cross-country. I was about halfway down the alley that goes behind the Village Smithy and Ruby

Holgate's house when I saw the fire truck come roaring out of the station. Fergie was just climbing aboard, so I dug deep and poured on the coal. The truck had to briefly slow down to make the corner at the old jail, and that's where I made my move.

I was throwing gravel as I cut between two cars and jumped for the rail. The truck was moving about 15 or 20 miles an hour and the momentum spun me around the rail and onto the deck. Fergie grabbed my arm until I could get squared away and off we went. Before we got to the railroad tracks, we had our hats on and were squinting into the wind.

I didn't realize it until later, but my second near miss could've ended up as a serious road rash. This time I made an error in judgement and lost at least a minute while Charlie Oliver's wife chewed me out for running through her flowers. I was trying to be polite and quickly re-planted the damaged bed while she went through her rendition of "And I thought you were such a nice boy."

I had lost valuable time and the truck was already up to speed. I was running for all I was worth. Fergie and my brother were reaching down from the fire truck, cheering me on, but I needed a break to come my way. I was starting to tire and my chances were getting slim.

I always hated those railroad tracks. The pavement wasn't real smooth where they crossed the street, and it provided a natural speed bump. Today the gave me the opportunity I needed. As the driver briefly slowed down for the tracks, I closed in and was pulled aboard.

As the years passed, we still occasionally got the chance to help with a fire. All of the regular firemen knew us and appreciated the help, but there was a regulation that you had to be eighteen to be an official member of the fire department. Soon enough we were of driving age, so we could at least get to the fires if we wanted to, but we still couldn't be official members of the town's finest.

One day we were driving our jeeps up on White Hill above town, when we suddenly noticed some smoke. We drove over to the fire to take a look. The dump was on fire and no one was around—nobody.

"The fire departmentshould be here pretty soon. Maybe we can help put it out," Stony said.

"To heck with them," I grumbled. "If they won't let us join, they don't need our help."

What had started as a dump fire was rapidly becoming a major problem. The immediate area was covered with pinyon/juniper forest, and we knew from experience that if those pitch-filled trees catch on fire, it gets fast and furious.

"Let's go report it," I said. We tore off for town in a cloud of dust.

The fire siren was hooked to the telephone. If anyone called in, the siren would ring until one of the volunteers came in to answer the phone and shut it off. We stopped at the nearest phone and called it in. The siren came in right on cue. We jumped back in our jeeps and soon we were standing around in front of the fire house waiting for the firemen to show up.

Here they came, flying from all over town. The first one to the fire station was the mayor, Odie Cooper. Odie threw the door open and picked up the phone. Of course no one was on the other end because we were standing right in front of him, and we had made the call. I pushed to the front of the crowd and blurted out, "We saw the fire, Odie. We called it in."

Odie said, "I'm sorry, but we're not going to let you guys ride the truck anymore. We had a meeting with our insurance man, and it seems the only people who are covered on our insurance policy are the card-carrying members of the fire department."

We protested, "You mean we can't help with the fires anymore?"

"That's what I mean, just get out of the way." Odie was starting to get cranky.

I never did like Odie. He never grew a decent garden and he was so cheap that he wouldn't pay any of us to mow his lawn. Ever since his son, Gordon, went up in space, Odie had been too good for everyone else in town. Gordon was one of the original Mercury astronauts. Sometimes, on Potato Day, Gordon would buzz the rodeo grounds with his fighter jet. It made the horses go crazy. Us kids even cleaned out the store next to the bakery and made it the

Gordon Cooper Public Library. Now Odie was saying we couldn't ride the fire truck anymore.

I walked up and looked at Odie. "So we can't ride the truck, huh, Odie?"

"That's right."

"Okay, then, we're not going to tell you where the fire is. I wouldn't worry too much about it, though, you'll be able to see the smoke in an hour or so."

"If you saw the fire, you have to tell us where it is." Odie was startin' to turn red.

"If we can't ride the truck, we're not going to tell you."

Odie kicked the ground and growled while most of the other firemen stood behind the truck and laughed. We had him, and he knew it.

"Okay," he relented, "but this is the last time, and I mean it."

I shot through the door and grabbed the chalk. I carefully wrote the exact location on the blackboard as Stony and Fergie moved our jeeps out of the driveway. Lighthearted firemen were loading up and Odie was driving the truck. No running this time, no-sirree-bob. I stepped up on the back of that old truck and grabbed myself a fireman's hat just like I knew what I was doing.

It was our last time. We were permanently banned from riding the truck or taking part in fighting fires. Even a manure fire was off limits to us. Odie never did forgive me for embarrassing him like that in front of all his underlings. Oh, well, he never got elected again, either.

And what do I want to be when I grow up?

Well, maybe a gardener.

Maybe I'll raise apples.

Maybe I'll put in a car wash...naw, that'll never work. Nobody will pay money to wash their own car...that's what they have kids for.

Heck, who knows. After learning how to handle those dogs when I was jumping through their back yards, maybe I'll become a dog trainer.

Within the heart of the Blue Grouse,
Lies the legend of the mountain spirit
for those who seek it.
I can easily close my eyes and visualize bird dogs
Stretching out across the open parks
of the Colorado high country.

The Shooter

Today I said goodbye to Bob Perigo. Bob is a clay target shooter, a champion, a teacher... a friend. As I watched his old Suburban wind off the ranch, rolling clouds of dust allowed a faint impression before spinning upward. I found myself being drawn into the turbulence until memories of our friendship became vivid and lasting. I suddenly was remembering a day, the day before I met Bob.

The false light of pre-dawn wasn't much help as I groped around in the tack shed hoping to come up with my saddle, a suitable hackamore, and a couple of horse hair pads.

Actually, it wasn't all that big a problem. Once you've used a certain riggin' for a time, you can tell if you have the right one just by touching it. I checked to make sure the pads were dry and drug the whole works into the catch pen where the horses were munching on breakfast and doing some light-hearted sparring. I recognized a friendly face and threw my saddle on him. "You're still interested in going with me this mornin', aren't you?" I brushed my glove along the underside of his belly so I could pick up the cinch strap on the other side. "It ain't like you've got a say in the matter, but it would sure be nice if you were coming out of want to."

"I'm getting started a little late," I thought to myself as I zipped my chaps on and walked my horse out of the corral.

"I don't know how I get myself into these things. You talk about cutting it close, I've got exactly six weeks to somehow transform this beat-up old cattle ranch into a believable upland bird hunting venue." My horse whipped me in the back with his tail as he nudged ahead to test the grass just beyond the rein's restriction. I don't think he fully understood the gravity of my situation. Even if he did, it didn't appear to bother him one way or the other. He leaned on me and pushed me forward a few steps.

I snugged up the reins and stepped aboard. He pulled one last mouthful of brome grass and we headed for the high country. Seems like I always do my best thinking while I take in as much of the Rocky Mountains as my day allows.

All in all I had the makin's of a great day; the weather was half decent, the quakies were in full color, and I was sitting on the best horse I was ever fortunate enough to end up with. He was a dandy dark sorrel quarter horse gelding. I always figured he liked the high country as much as I did because he didn't like to waste much time gettin' there. I favor a horse who will step out and walk, one who will work at it.

We had no sooner swung out onto the trail when his lower neck and flanks started to darken with sweat. He lowered his head a little as he looked at a downed log then stepped over it and slipped into his walking gait. Today we would be riding the upper fence line. We would stay with it most of the day before dropping back down into the fields this evening.

They say this park I'm riding through used to be an old Ute Indian racetrack although it looks pretty much like any of the smaller parks in this brush country. There doesn't seem to be any distinguishing marks and the grass combinations are identical to the area around it. Anyway, legend has it that the Indians used it as a racetrack for many years.

My uncle Alden told me a whole herd of cattle mysteriously died here in this same field one fall. I touched my horse's mane with the back of my glove. "Seems like there should be some old bones around or something if all that was going on up here," I told him.

It wasn't like the Indians didn't leave anything behind; this country is almost famous for holding artifacts. Every homesteader who laid stake around here found plenty; flint arrowheads, beads, and pottery. They say my grampa's ranch would cough up a whole new crop of arrowheads and beads after a hard rain. I carefully checked out the anthills as I rode past. Many times you can pick up a handful of beads in a single hill. I knew where there were a couple of burial grounds, and I would pass by a series of Indian caves later on in the day.

My horse stretched his neck to pull a little slack in the rein and ducked under an oak brush limb. I instinctively leaned down over the saddle horn and shielded my head with my gloves while I held my hat on. This oak brush is the most dominant shrub species found in the transition zone between the pinyon/juniper forest of the foothills and the timber of the Colorado alpines.

I guess it's technically called "Gambel's oak," but you might get run off the ranch for saying it. During this time of year the oak brush is quickly losing its leaves. Hardwood leaves are always stunning in autumn but the color lasts for oh-so-brief a time. I've always figured that the oak brush gets kind of a raw deal, naturally speaking, when it comes to its leaves. The oaks only get to keep their foliage during the summer months. They are just about the last to finally leaf out in the spring, and one of the very first to drop their leaves in the fall. As nice as it is to have the oaks in full bloom, it would be some better if they stuck around a little longer. Oak brush is a very good habitat base. Mix in a little serviceberry, chokecherry, and a healthy dose of big sagebrush and you've got the quality fixin's for every wildlife species that has fastened itself to this lifestyle.

We climbed out on top of a gorgeous bench; you talk about your ringside seat. This bench affords maybe the best view I've ever seen in this mountain country. The bench is actually a pretty typical alluvial fan, the soil is a little rocky at the base but grows deeper and more fertile as it spreads out and drops slightly in elevation. Rich combinations of alpine grass, legumes and forbs crowd together along the edges of this natural theatre. I hopped off my horse and walked beside him. I don't like to hurry across here. Several years ago I named this place "Archie's Manor" in honor of my father. I prefer to walk through the Manor, that way I get to spend just a little more time in thought, paying my respects the only way I truly know how.

I don't really care where you spend most of your time, somewhere along the way, sometime in every day, water becomes a consideration. Water is the center of the universe and I don't think you'll get any argument from one single living species on earth. With it, you're in the groove, without it you're dead. I decided to drop into the West Mesa Creek drainage.

I braced each hand on a rock as I lowered my chest to the damp black clay of the creek-bank. I waited until half-a-dozen quakie leaves floated past before I touched my lips to the water. Out of the corner of my eye I saw my horse pulling deep just three feet off my right shoulder.

I love to watch horses drink, they seem to enjoy it more than most animals. They will usually tuck one shoulder and slightly bend a knee to make drinking more comfortable. Somehow it made me feel good to know that he and I were sharing this ribbon of life...touching it together.

I pushed myself up and knelt down on one knee beside him. I rubbed my hand along the wet hair covering his cannon bone and breathed as deeply as I could. There's nothing on earth that smells better than a sweaty horse, at least nothing I've ever run across.

"Now don't be tanking up on me," I warned him. "It's only a thousand or so feet before we break out on top but I don't want you getting sick." A guy's got to be careful when he's watering his stock. If you give them a little every now and then, you're pretty much good to go all day, but if you let them get hot and tired before giving them a drink, they will usually draw in too much and never seem to get it all taken care of. They spend most of the day looking for more water. It's just like a guy who's been broke all his life suddenly coming into a pile of money. Within a few short weeks he's pretty much back where he started from and all he got out of it was a sick feeling in his stomach. Take it from me, that feeling hangs around a little longer than you'd like.

We followed the creek for another half a mile before easing out into a little basin. The basin is actually the fountainhead of the creek. Rich, boggy mud coated the first foot or so of my horses' legs as we circled a shallow pond choked with algae and pond weed. Five elk moved out ahead of us into a thick quakie forest. I couldn't tell if they were bulls or cows, but their rumps were broad and their coats shiny. We stopped at the edge of the park as I scoured the woods for more elk. Quakie leaves were floating and swirling on a light breeze, several rattling to rest on my hat and shoulders.

I slid out of the saddle and stood alongside my horse while I checked his cinches and breast collar. I reached up to pull his forelock from beneath the leather of the headstall when I caught a glimpse of something moving on the other side of the horse. I slowly peeked under his throat latch, between his head and neck, to see a large bull elk standing less than ten yards from us.

A nice five-point bull with about half of his velvet rubbed off. Strips of fuzzy velvet were dangling near his brow tines. I didn't move, he didn't move, and the horse didn't move for several minutes.

Finally the bull ambled away, his eyes blinking rapidly, his nose testing his fortune with every heartbeat. There are a few animals, like skunks, javelina, mule deer, and elk that carry with them a distinctive, unmistakable aroma.

It's like a pretty girl who smiles as she brushes by you, briefly looks into your eyes, and then disappears into the crowd. As you lean to look where she went, her fragrance settles in around you and leaves you wishing you'd have come up with something brilliant to say. I closed my eyes and breathed in the lingering essence of this magnificent animal. Is it similar to Chanel or Estée Lauder? Naw, it's actually elk urine, sprinkled generously on the dark under-hair of his stomach, but it's marvelous just the same.

"You know, he just walked away," I whispered. "I'm not so sure he ever really saw us. One thing's sure enough, old buddy, something like that will get your heart started. Whew." I swung on and headed into the quakies. If I hadn't been paying attention before, I sure as hell would be now.

It takes about three hours to cross the top of the ranch property. Most of it ends up being thick quakies with some holdings of brush, a few small parks and scattered fir from time to time. A few springs drop out of this high country to do what they can to help with the water problems down below. I had plenty of time to think about my project so I focused on my priorities while my horse strutted through the woods like he owned 'em.

My shooting dog program was solid, up and running, and the old hay fields were doing a fairly decent job of holding up their end of the stick. Overall the habitat was bearable and the construction of the infrastructure was coming along well. We were about a third of the way into our water management plan, so with any luck, we should be ready to open on schedule.

There was one thing that had been bothering me. I'd been putting it off for a couple of months now. I'd promised the owner we would have our clay target shooting program squared away for the opening.

We planned to start with traditional trap and skeet and later finishing the sporting clay courses. The concrete contractor had been telling me of a friend of his who was supposed to be a terrific shooter, someone who had the expertise to assist me in developing a top quality layout. I always hate it when someone starts promoting a friend of a friend.

You know how it goes: Oh, I know this guy who used to work for my uncle Harvey. Every now and then he and ol' Harvey would go night fishing with this friend of his from Utah. Apparently this guy had a close friend who figured out how to make whiskey out of potato peels. He sells it to the townies and claims to make pretty good money at it. I guess for a little cash down he'll set you up in business and all you have to pay him is 25% of your take. The whole deal is about half legal and the guy's supposed to be honest as the day is long.

Well of course my situation wasn't quite as bad as that but I still felt a little uneasy about bringing a new face into the mix at this stage of the game. One thing was for sure, I needed the help and the guy lived just upriver from me. What could it hurt to at least talk to him. I decided to call him first thing in the morning. Right, wrong, or indifferent we needed to get the target shooting venue off the ground.

I pulled up to a wire gate that looked like it had been stretched with a D-9 cat. Some of those old ranchers took a lot of pride in building gates that flat couldn't be opened without cutting your arm or tearing your shirt. I believe it was like sport to them. I wouldn't be surprised if they sat back in the woods and laughed at every unfortunate soul who tried to pry that wire over the gate post. I squeezed the gate post into my right shoulder and cussed under my breath as one of the barbs sunk to the hilt in the skin of my chest. "We ought to just leave the damned thing down," I told the horse as he spun through the opening and turned to watch me wrestle with it again. "There's just no sense in building a gate..." I was halfway through my complaining when my ride walked out from under me while I was still climbing on. Horses don't mind listening to all your problems but they take offense at your bitching about such a little thing as opening a gate, especially when they figure they're doing the lion's share of the work out there.

We took a little jog around some lava rocks and started into a shady spot in the trail. All of the sudden he threw his head up, humped, tucked his butt a little and bounced down the trail about 15 yards or so. I spun in the saddle to find out what had startled him.

At first I thought a sharp limb had poked him in the flanks or maybe he caught some brush up under his tail. No such luck; while I was turned in the saddle, he bogged his head and blew up. Down through the timber we went, him trying to prove a point, me trying to talk him out of it. My dad always warned me about bailing out of these situations. "I don't care what it looks like, kid, stay on him. Your chances of getting hurt are a lot greater if you try to get off while things are fast and furious." It turns out that these were great words of wisdom concerning many things. When life spins you out of control, stay in there. Don't get jumpy, stay with the ship. In all probability, things aren't quite as bad as they look, stay focused and ride it out.

Sometimes it wasn't all that easy followin' Dad's advice. I grabbed the saddle horn and picked up as much weight as I could in my stirrups. "What the hell...ugh, chuh. I guess you couldn't have done this while we were down in the pasture, you dirty bastard." A pine branch swatted me in the face sending my sunglasses into a pretty arc over my head. "That's it," I gritted, "if my glasses get broke out of this deal you and I are going to have it out." About that time my right thigh starting burning. I glanced down to see either a yellowjacket or a ground bee all hunkered down, stinging me for all he was worth. Things were looking up, at least I now knew why I was being thrown around like a rag doll. This wasn't anything personal, we had ridden through a swarm of bees and he was catching it in a big way on his stomach and under his rear quarters.

I finally took up enough slack in the reins to pull his head up and turned him uphill. When the dust cleared, I tied him up to a serviceberry bush and found myself backtracking. I was doing my best to work out a major crick in my lower back while I searched for my sunglasses and flexed the cramps out of my knees.

The bees were still strafing the ground and swarming the immediate vicinity of the wreck so I snagged my sunglasses and jumped over a log before sprinting down to my horse who was throttling the air as he danced from side to side, swishing his tail in defiance.

I led him down the trail a couple hundred yards, and after a quick once-over, hopped back on. We were just above an old reservoir so I cut through some sparse timber and dropped into the lake at the inlet. I rode him out into the water until my boots filled up and sat there with my eyes closed while the muddy water calmed his welts. "I'm sorry I called you a dirty bastard back there," I apologized. He lifted his head and shook from one end to the other. I slouched back in the saddle and cozied to the sun on my face.

The evening light was glowing as it lay across the upper fields of the ranch. I was singing while we stood on a rocky bluff overlooking the northeast corner of the property. I can't speak for all animals but dogs and horses love music. Singing is a secret passion of mine so many times they have patiently tolerated my rendition of one song or another while they lounged in the shade and rested tired muscles.

"Let's roll it up," I said, as I draped the reins over the swells of the saddle and started walking down the trail. He dobbed his head enough to feel comfortable with the slack and followed along. I wasn't going to get any argument from him, it was time to call it good.

We walked together until the soft soil of the hayfield cushioned his hooves. I loaded up and tapped him into a lope. His midday lather was dry now and the cool air of the evening swept his enthusiasm homeward. I laid my right hand on the muscles of his front shoulder. They were rippling, hard, like they were cut from stone. Just think of it, eleven hundred pounds of energy and power, taking me home. How? Swiftly, with enduring style. Why? Because I asked him. What a marvelous creature, this horse. What a monumental moment in life, this day.

I was working a couple of pointers near the ranch entrance the following morning when I saw the cement contractor rambling up the lane. Just behind him, out of his dust, appeared an old gray International Scout. Truthfully, I heard it before I saw it. The old rig was laboring down the road rattling its disapproval of our new road-base.

"Must be that hotshot shooter I've been hearing about," I said to myself. "That car looks like something I'd buy. Oh well, I won't hold that against him." I whistled my dogs near and walked toward the barns where most of the staff, the contractor and his friend were milling about. Even from a distance this new guy stuck out like a sore thumb. He had to be at least six foot five, maybe even taller.

I walked up and shook some hands before one of the kennel helpers took the dogs off their leads and jumped them into the dog trailer. The shooter wasn't talking much, he had a serious look on his face and his demeanor wasn't friendly. His long gray hair was pulled back into a pony tail that fluffed down below his shoulders. He sported a splendid thick mustache, one of those handlebar types.

He was wearing an old brown sweater with several holes in the sleeves and cuffs. The inseams of those jeans had to be at least 38 inches long. He was lean and lanky and walked with a smooth stride that fairly caressed the ground as he passed over.

He was wearing a new green cap with "Classic Doubles" embroidered in gold letters across the front. An old leather belt was cranked down around his waist and held fast by a large, silver, oval-shaped buckle. "High Overall Champion" was embossed in the silver. His eyes were hidden behind expensive amber shaded shooting glasses. His face was drawn and ruddy. Cigarette smoke boiled out of his mouth and his voice was deep and gravelly as he began. "Name's Bob Perigo," he announced. "I hear you're looking for someone who can help you with your clay target operation."

"Yes sir," I replied. "You got some time to talk it over?"

"I'm training for a big upcoming shoot this afternoon, why don't you come down to the club and we'll hash it over while I shoot a few rounds?"

"Sounds good to me, Bob, I'll meet you down there later."

I walked him over to his car. I must have been staring as I thought to myself, "Looks like he and this old Scout both have a lot of miles on them."

He crawled into the driver's seat and closed the door. The car door was held shut by a chrome hasp, you know, like a gate latch. I guess it could be kind of handy, if you wanted to put a padlock on your car door. He ground away on the old starter until the engine reluctantly fired up, then disappeared behind dirt and road film as he rolled his window up and drove away.

Stick around, there's a lot more to this fellow and I'd surely appreciate it if you let me tell you about him. He impacted my life and the lives of my children like no other.

Bob Perigo was a shooter, so it only seemed fittin' to meet him on his turf, to see him in action. That's where our friendship started; me watching him shoot international skeet under the capable guidance of his mentor and coach, Andy Young. He shot four rounds that afternoon and ground up 98 of the 100 targets he called for.

Okay, so the guy could shoot, but that's not what impressed me as I sat on the ground and leaned back against the trunk of a big riverbank cottonwood tree. I observed an amazing transition that afternoon. He was all business as he loaded the machines with targets and prepared for his regular workout. He joked a little with Andy while he pulled his gear from the backseat of the old Scout but when he unsnapped his gun case he changed before my eyes.

You see, Bob never had any kids, at least none he ever told me about. As he assembled his shotgun it became apparent that this gun was as a child to him. He thoughtfully stroked it and admired it from one end to the other. It reminded me of a caring mother, dressing her children in the morning. You sometimes see fly fishermen consumed by a similar vision as they lovingly rig their favorite rod. Everything had to be just so before he broke it open and tucked it under his right arm.

He lit a cigarette and quietly accommodated Andy's instruction as he pulled his hat down tight, adjusted his glasses and looked out toward the mountains. This was a different man than I had met just hours before at the ranch. He was now enthused and excited, soft and collected.

I witnessed the surfacing of his passion, the dreams of his heart, an aura of gentleness tempered with gritty determination and obvious structure.

Bob had a definitive confidence in his voice as he strode onto the first station and called for his targets. "Paaall," he growled, a mighty statement instead of a wish, or request. I always loved Bob's trademark call, the utterance of a single word that challenged all within earshot. "If you're going to win today, you're going to have to beat me to do it."

Bob had grown up a military kid and it showed through in just about everything he did. His speech was very direct, his voice resembled that of a drill sergeant.

You know, I've always looked up to folks who willingly put it all on the line to achieve their personal dreams of success—someone who will dig it out, day after week after month after year. Just about everything Bob owned was thrown in the back of that old Scout of his. He didn't have a house or property. He didn't have a career, or even a steady job for that matter. Every dime he could scrape up went into his shooting. He had sacrificed his soul and all that goes with it for a moment in time where he could stand alone at the top of his game.

Sure there were many championships; sure there were great victories over the course of his extended effort, but, as is true in many of our lives, the one goal that stood above all others had eluded him, maybe forever. He laid awake nights dreaming of the day when he would stand on center stage, the Olympic gold medal for International Skeet swinging from his neck. He damn near made the U.S. Team on two separate occasions, something he never quite got over.

Although he was an All American sporting clay shooter and continually hovered with the best in the business at every shoot he attended, for some reason he could never deal with what he considered to be the dominating failure in his life. Of the millions of clay targets he turned to powder, there were a handful of misses that weighed unfairly in his mind, at least to my way of thinkin'.

"This is a guy I can work with," I decided. "This is a guy I can trust."

Andy kidded him about missing two birds as Bob and I shared a cold pepsi and worked through the residual uneasiness that always accompanies meeting someone new.

"We might as well get started on that target range, Bob," I said as I stood to leave.

"How's tomorrow sound to you. I'll clear it with the boss this evening."

It turned out that Bob knew every detail of a skeet and trap field like he knew the worn-out clutch in his car. He had memorized every distance, every measurement, every angle, every elevation. This made things remarkably simple for me. Once we selected a suitable site, all I had to do was get out of the way and let him build it. Within a month of our meeting, we were laying sod and doing final touch-up on a shooting layout that stirred the soul of every individual who walked onto it.

My project came out of the blocks right on schedule and for the next two years, Bob stayed at the helm, as our range master and personal instructor. He managed a few shoots along the way but his total dedication was to the integrity of our collective effort.

Although we provided top-end bird hunting and a dog operation without peer, the most frequent compliment was referring to Bob's teaching. He was especially adept at working with young people and ladies.

There is a fascinating process ingrained in developing recreational opportunity for the wealthy. This process involves the start-up, or building phase; the ascension phase; the realization phase; and unfortunately a stage of decline. Somewhere between ascension and realization is where the owner feels a need to take over and prominent professionals in the business are replaced by middle-of-the-road bean counters who are content to bask in the glory of someone else's hard work. It seems unfair the first couple of times you go through it, but looking back, it pretty much has to happen that way.

Within the short span of two years, we had completed the transformation of a bankrupt cattle ranch into a world-class shooting venue. I got the news on the first of February that I'd worn out my welcome. While I was gathering my stuff and saying my goodbyes to probably the best staff I've ever seen, I received a call on the radio from the target range. Bob ask me to come over before I headed out. I drove over to the range for the last time that morning and talked with Bob. He was obviously upset about the changes occurring on the ranch and was visibly shaken at my leaving. We searched for words and grasped for composure while we stood together outside the range clubhouse on that chilly February morning. We shook hands.

"I'll see you down the road, buddy," I said finally, as I climbed back into the jeep and started to drive away. After driving only a few yards, I stopped to look back. Bob was standing at attention, holding his right hand in a salute. Tears were rolling down his cheeks as he summoned his inimitable voice. "It's been a pleasure, Cap'n."

"Indeed it has, my friend, indeed it has," I answered.

Bob buckled down and gritted out the next year and a half as the place slid into inevitable decline. The dog program left with me and the hunts became more and more infrequent until financial pressure collapsed the project, eclipsing all of our efforts, individual and cooperative.

In the meantime, I had gathered my second wind and fired up a new wildlife project just ten miles down river. I was back in the groove, training, selling dogs, hunting birds and fishing. I liked this place but most of all I liked the fact that no one was looking over my shoulder. I made the decisions and took the heat if they didn't turn out.

There was only one thing missing, really, a sporting clay range. I didn't want to build a traditional trap and skeet layout. Everyone wanted to shoot sporting and it was a heck of a lot cheaper to build and maintain.

Once again, enter Bob Perigo. Before either of us knew it, we were measuring, staking, cutting trails and ordering machines. It was just like old times. His schedule started filling up giving lessons and running the day-to-day operation of the range. This time there was no money-man behind us so we had to make solid decisions based on cash flow.

My sons, Bryce and Jayme, were starting to shoot quite a bit by then. Bryce was ten and Jayme was eight years old. They had spent their entire lives following me around so they had a pretty good idea how I like things done. At eight years of age Jayme was filling his days with everything from fishing to baseball but Bryce liked the looks of that sporting clay range. He started helping Bob by toting cases of targets and adjusting machines. He picked up spent hulls and cleaned up around the stations, that is, until he got his chance to shoot.

Bryce had been shooting birds in training for several years so he had a leg up on most kids his age. He was shooting a twenty-gauge 1100 most of the time, and anything he could grab for the rest of it. Bob liked what he saw in the boy and politely asked me if he could accompany him to tournaments within the state. Of course I agreed.

Under Bob's thoughtful tutorage, Bryce won everything short of a National Championship over the next three years. He started by burning the other youth competitors in our immediate area and stunned many of the men shooters in the process. When he was eleven, he won silver medals in the National Championship and the Pan American Games. He ended up on three All American teams, won six state titles, three regional and zone championships, and numerous sanctioned events.

Bob quietly stood in the background while famous shooters from all over the world took their share of the credit for Bryce's success. Granted, many people helped out along the way—some with ammunition, some with lessons, and some with custom gun work. He was a fearless young shooter. Nothing shook him. He was Bob's true protégé, fashioned for success. I would sometimes grin in silence as I saw him revert to Bob's training when things were going rough for him.

There were times during major shoots when I worried about Bryce's state of mind; that is, until I saw him bear down, leaning on his structure. When he knew he needed to finish strong you could hear his young voice call to his training. Louder, and more confident he would bark, "Paall." When he started doing that, I didn't know who would end up winning second, but I knew who was gonna win first.

Although Jayme seemed occupied by other interests, he took wonderful advantage of his natural style and won the Wing Sport tournament going away. I saw him go three full seasons without missing a grouse. He has developed into a fabulous basketball player and his depth of character is amazing for his age. Even now, six years later, both of my boys are gleaning benefits from their time with Bob Perigo.

Because Bob has a shooter's heart, he designs beautiful courses–courses for the shooter. Sure there are lots of great shooters out there. Sure there are lots of other instructors out there. They wear all the latest gear and fly from one place to the next. They rent swank hotel rooms and drive rental cars. They are all certified instructors, a fact they will remind you of every time they get a chance. The last I heard Bob still hadn't got certified. He thought it too demeaning. He did finally take the old Scout out in the back yard and shot it in the head. He picked up an aging Suburban and pressed on in the only way he knew how.

If you're attending a major shoot, you know, trying to make your mark, and you see a flashback from the early seventies come staggering out of the high house on the skeet range. He was sleeping in there. He had to, you see, he had every last cent tied up in his entry fee. He fended for himself last night while you and your buddies were eating high on the hog and toasting to your success. He might look like he went in that house sometime around 1970 and just came out today. His hair might be pulled back in a long gray pony tail. I'll be willing to bet a year's wages he'll be wearing an old wool sweater with holes around the elbows and cuffs. His hands shake a little now when he lights his cigarettes or drinks his coffee.

He's probably got just enough ammunition to warm up and shoot the event. He'll worry about gas money for the trip home later. He's a master at the shuck and jive. He's my friend and I'm damn proud of it.

I'll let you in on another little secret while I'm at it. I've stood beside World Champions, European Champions, British and French Open Champions, International Live Pigeon Champions, U.S. Champions, Olympic gold medalists, All Americans and everyone in between. I've seen courses designed by the best in the business, and I've paid good money for lessons from top-level instructors.

I believe Bob Perigo to be the best pure shooter I've ever known. You see, he competes because there is nothing else his soul will settle for. He never caved in, never compromised. He has repeatedly sacrificed everything that is commonly held dear by others to try again, just one more time. You can bet when he steps in there and gasses it up, you'll have to beat him to win. When he's on he'll be in the top squad almost every time.

Yes, today our lives again took different roads. Today I said goodbye.

I seriously doubt if I will ever be involved with shooting sports again. Because of that, I may never get the chance to work with Bob, or even visit for that matter. Having said that, I want to leave you with this sincere and heartfelt thought.

I've been in the company of thousands of shooters in my day but when that one question comes up, "Who was the best you ever saw?" My answer is obvious.

If you're thinking of building a new clay target course, or if you are finally getting around to arranging for lessons for you or your family, do yourself a favor. Take a trip to Aspen, Colorado, and ask around until you find where Bob is hanging out. Tell him Mike Gould says hello. A tip of the hat to you, old friend. And on behalf of my sons...Thanks.

The Thorns of the Valley

The first time I saw the Camas Prairie of north-central Idaho, I was both inspired and amazed. I'd grown up in the capable embrace of the Rocky Mountains, but I had no idea they held such a magnificent secret treasure safely between the drainages of the Salmon and Clearwater Rivers.

Idaho's backcountry is so rugged, there is only one state highway that winds its way from south to north. I'm sure the folks who planned and constructed that highway did the best they could, but even so, the road maneuvers through a couple of Indian nations and at least one other state before entering Canada at the narrows of Idaho.

No matter the season, it's best to be prepared for anything if you're planning to take on that particular stretch of pavement. I've been down through there many times, and I've seen just about every kind of nastiness Mother Nature has in her bag of surprises. Twice I've barely gotten my rig shut down in time to see massive rockslides cover the entire road just north of Riggins. I've pushed through snowslides and inched over two hundred miles of black ice so wonderfully glassy that you could have held the Olympic figure skating championships on it at any given point.

One New Year's Eve, somewhere around midnight, a state

highway worker and I watched as at least a third of a mile of Highway 95 washed into the raging floodwaters of the Little Salmon River just above New Meadows. After retreating back upriver to New Meadows, I learned that similar landslides had occurred on the Weiser and Payette Rivers, and the long and short of it was, I was trapped. Six bird dogs and I spent the next five days watching houses, barns, cattle and personal belongings float by us on their way from wherever they started from to somewhere between us and the Pacific Ocean.

Just before dawn on the sixth day, I eased through the Little Salmon River and made a break for it. The water was still deep enough to cover my headlights, and the rising water level on the floorboard of the truck kept me from lingering too long worrying about whether the road was still under me or not. The pointer sitting beside me on the seat looked at me like I was nuts. I'm sure he secretly wondered if the windows were rolled up tight enough to give us time to get to the other side. We made it across the bridge, and after a 550-mile detour over backroads and logging skids, we finally pulled into the house.

What keeps me coming back? What is it that makes the whole process worthwhile? Well, for me, it's a combination of the unbelievable majesty of the canyons, the rich cultural heritage of the Nez Perce Nation, the spectacular and powerful rivers, and of course, the jewel of the North—the Camas Prairie.

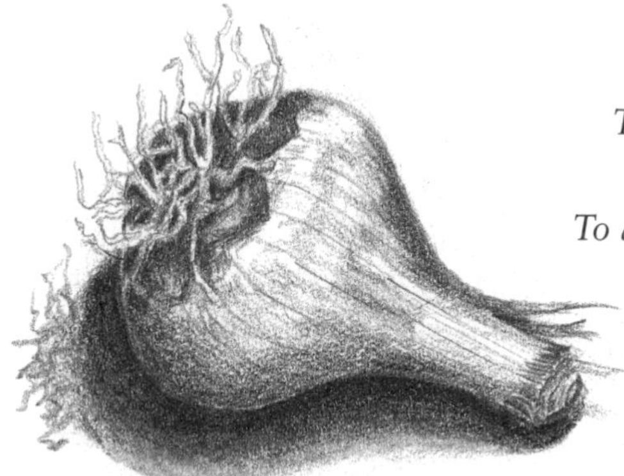

The Camas lily takes the blue
from the sky each spring,
To add grace and decoration to the
expansive grasslands.

The prairie is named for the native camas lily that once brought the blue from the sky each spring to add grace and decoration to the expansive grasslands. As is true throughout the natural world, the camas flower also had a very practical application. The camas bulbs were collected, prepared, and stored as an important winter staple of the Indian diet.

Nowadays, only remnants of the flowers are visible each spring, as the ultra-rich volcanic soil of the prairie is divided into an elaborate system of modern-day farms that resemble a grand patchwork quilt of bright greens, yellows and browns. The rolling prairie stretches out until finally, it gently gives way to the river canyons that seem to hold it up. It's like a rich pedestal, an extremely fertile blanket of black topsoil that gladly accepts abundant annual precipitation and, in return, rewards those whose labor is expended in its behalf by yielding bushel-per-acre crops that flatland farmers can only dream of.

They say the prairie was formed ten or twelve million years ago as a result of volcanic activity over in the Columbia Basin of Washington. All of this makes sense if you take a little time to study the rock formations and the deep, black soil.

Now, I'm not a farmer, and although I admire the work of those folks who put it all on the line year after year out there, I have come to appreciate the prairie for an entirely different reason. For some reason, the Idaho Fish and Game Department decided to do their first official release of pheasant near the little town of Kamiah sometime just after the turn of the century. Later on came chukar partridge, Hungarian partridge, wild turkey and valley quail.

Those upland game birds took to that country like green to grass. For many years, the southern edge of the Camas Prairie was known as "Pheasant Central" in Idaho. The cheat grass that was introduced by stockmen along the rugged river canyons kept the chukar in hog heaven, while the transition zones between the cropland and the canyons were all the Hungarians needed to set up permanent shop. Valley quail prefer brushy draws and valley floors, so they, too, found what they needed to sustain themselves, and to this day, bountiful populations are everywhere the habitat is suitable.

The dense evergreen forests of north-central Idaho hold literally millions of ruffed, spruce, and blue grouse, and have proven to be the ideal habitat for flourishing wild turkey families.

When you take into consideration the human population is best described as scant and those that are there are quality, hard-working, decent folks who have yet to deny me permission to run my bird dogs on their land, and the town is clean, caring, and virtually void of crime and commercialization—I figured I had hit the mother lode.

For the past four years, I've rented a run-down farm nine miles from town, and have walked thousands of miles in study of this remarkable natural wonder that the Nez Perce Nation was nice enough to allow the federal government to steal from them. I have become very fond of their tradition and consider my Indian friends some of the finest people I've ever been close to.

There have been many memorable times and personal contacts with wildlife that could not have occurred anywhere else in the lower 48 states, but this story specifically documents one of the most powerful moments in a lifetime of study.

One morning early last fall, I set out from the house with two young pointing dogs with the intention of scouting partridge coveys along the rim of the Cottonwood Creek Canyon. The plan was to loop a couple of miles to the southeast, and then follow the canyon until a wide drainage came in from the north. I would then cross the drainage and circle back toward home. I guessed the walk would be somewhere around seven miles. I should be home by noon to take care of the rest of the stock, I thought.

I tapped the dogs off and stood to watch their initial race to the front. This has become a custom of mine. It sets my mind into motion and allows my heart to soften and become receptive.

Each of these walks is much like a movie you've been dying to see. Movie-makers have mastered the skill of setting their patrons in place with beautiful music specifically composed to set the mood for the upcoming event. If the movie is to represent a story of love and life, the music is soft and reflective. These orchestrations apprehend your spirit and cause you to immediately sense and recall those things that you love and admire the most in your life.

I saw plumes of dew rising from the pasture grass as my dogs cut swirling seams into the never-ending arcs of their future. They were running side by side as they reached the opposite end of the field and jumped the fence in unison.

I stared into the mist that hovered over the cropland as the music began in the theater of my mind. I was positively transfixed as I allowed my senses to swell with every breath. I could feel the timeless glory of creation, I could hear the music in my spirit, I could smell the fragrance of the season, and I could taste the elements of the air I was breathing.

While I continued to scan the horizon, I felt my pockets for the necessities and stepped through an invisible veil into a day I'll never forget.

My steps were particularly heavy this day. An overwhelming sadness was draped around my shoulders, and there was just no setting it down. One of life's certainties is that, sooner or later, each person has to face the loss of that which matters most. In my case, this was the unyielding realization that my wife had disappeared with the morning mist some months prior, and like the mist, some things are impossible to recreate. Sometimes we learn too late of mistakes we've made along the way, and often the universal laws of consequence are brutally permanent.

I could easily visualize her beauty and her smile as I ducked under the fence and struck out for a dilapidated homestead the dogs were obviously attracted to. I fought off the desire to return to the house and willed myself to quicken my pace and make the best of the situation.

The old homestead house had long since been reduced to its native rock foundation, but the barn was still holding on to some vague hope that the caring owner would someday return. A couple of rusty pieces of tin tapped together as a gentle southwestern wind pushed against the aging barn and persistently reminded it that the day was coming in which collapse was inevitable.

I found myself focusing on the barn as I approached and I mused about what we had in common, this barn and I, until I glanced beyond the structure to the yellow weeds near the edge of a barley field.

Rhythmic waves rippled through the waist-high barley to reveal my dogs standing tall and intense. They were bent into the wind, both looking down a slight incline into the weeds. I'm ashamed to admit it, but my heart wasn't in it this morning. I casually walked to their front, and was clearly out of position when a dozen or so Hungarians blasted out of the weeds and sailed down into a shallow ravine.

"Let's follow them up," I said to the dogs. "I promise I'll do a better job for you if you get them found again."

The dogs needed no further invitation. They sprinted away into a brushy bottom and set their course for the ravine. Now normally I try to keep the high ground so I can get a clear picture of what's going on out front, but embarrassed by my previous effort, I found myself entering the thicket on what appeared to be an old cattle trail.

I noticed a seeping spring had surfaced just above me, and the steep slope had the water accelerating into a small creek before I went a hundred yards into the brush. I reasoned that this was good because the day was really starting to heat up. It was going to get hot, and it would be nice and handy to have water for the dogs nearby.

Right away it became obvious that this was no run-of-the-mill patch of brush. There was a lot more to this ravine than I was prepared for—facts that soon became painfully apparent. First off, the brush was extremely dense, and the trail I was on offered meager benefit. Cows look like pretty big animals while they're out grazing in a pasture, but they're really not all that tall. The trail resembled more of a tunnel than anything else. It kept me bent over most of the time, and crawling on hands and knees for the rest of it.

If this wasn't bad enough, the draw was getting steeper and narrower, and everything down there had either thorns or stickers on it. I stopped to listen for the dogs for a minute and quietly took stock of my surroundings. I'd never seen so many varieties of thistle and thornbrush in one place in my life.

I noted hawthorne, wild rose, and blackberry bramble in abundance. There were healthy stands of Canadian, musk, bull and yellow star thistle. My chaps were successful in turning everything from my thighs down, but my T-shirt looked like I'd just run through a barbed-wire fence and both of my arms were scratched and bleeding from my gloves up. Even the short grass was mostly comprised of cheat and foxtail, so my socks were packed with irritating hawns too numerous to mess with.

I just wasn't in the mood for this. Of all days to end up in a jungle from hell, I mean...come on, now. I found myself getting frustrated and a penetrating funk was settling down on me. It's like when a skunk sprays your dog on the back porch—some things take time to wear out.

I wasn't too worried about the dogs. I knew they would be checking in with me soon. I no longer cared where the Huns ended up, either. I just felt a need to get the heck out of there.

Along the bottom of the draw, near the creek, there were some big old cottonwoods, dogwood, and several huge willow trees. It looked like some years before a vicious wind of some type had come through there and ripped substantial limbs from the trees leaving jagged deadfall everywhere. The entire scene was devilish in appearance, foreboding and spooky. Even the whitetail deer herd that scurried up the opposite hillside didn't give my spirit the usual lift. I could only guess the occasional whir of wings I heard were ruffed grouse. I never did see one, but they sure sounded like grouse to me.

All of the sudden I noticed a tree that didn't seem to fit. It was across the creek from me, and it looked strangely like a fruit tree. I scrambled across a large, dead cottonwood limb and pushed through the brush to the tree. It was a fruit tree, and it was loaded with apples. "Boy, that's weird," I thought to myself. "What an unbelievable place for an apple tree."

I yanked a couple of apples off the lower branches, more out of defiance than anything else, and started munching on one. The dogs came running by me with tongues and tails bleeding and flopped down in the dark mud of the creek. "It's good to see you guys," I told them. "I was beginning to long for some company down here." They didn't seem too interested, but I pointed to the apple tree and showed them the hard evidence I held in my hand.

"This thing can't get any worse, so let's take this trail down a

little further and see if we can catch a side trail that will take us up and out of this hell-hole. What do you say?"

They were all stretched out in the mud as I moved past them, but jumped up and followed me across the log back into the thickness. Just as I rejoined the trail, I saw fresh bear sign and a partial track in the mud. The sign was full of cherry pits, greenery, and something that looked like apricot or plum pits.

"Must be some chokecherries down here someplace," I said out loud. "There's bound to be some grouse around them if we can find them."

Ten yards down the trail I found more bear sign, and ten yards beyond that, another apple tree. This tree was different from the first. The apples were golden instead of red. This was amazing. Not only had I come across apples, but two different types. Pretty soon I stumbled on more apples, and then plums, then pears, then apricots. Everything was in season, so I picked and ate as I continued.

I didn't really mind getting my arms scratched up, and I didn't mind crawling every now and then, but getting my hat dragged off every five minutes was beginning to make me mad. I hate that.

After my hat got tangled in a hawthorne bush and fell to the ground for the umpteenth time, I took a wild swing at it and snatched it off the ground. Wait a minute—there were cherry pits all over the ground where my hat was laying. These weren't chokecherries like I'd thought. These were real cherry pits and they were everywhere.

I backed through a little opening in the brush and eased up on the hillside a little so I could see what the heck was going on. I looked up through the canopy of brush and above me some forty feet were the crowns of the biggest cherry trees I've ever seen, and they were laden with thousands of dark red cherries.

I couldn't stand it any longer. This was just too weird, too strange. I fought my way up the hill for another fifty yards and found the biggest patch of daylight I'd seen in over an hour. From there I could see the bigger picture. There were many fruit trees of all kinds down through that bottom, and now that I had some elevation, I could see them. I maneuvered over near a spring and sat down on a big rock.

For the next two hours, I sat on that rock and thought about my life. I was tired and bleeding, hot and frustrated. I was hurting terribly from the extended circumstances in my life. I had somehow managed to get through every obstacle that I'd encountered in my life, but had I finally come to a hill that was too steep to climb?

Many times, when a man loses his dream, he loses his will to live. Within the confines of that valley, I'd come to that invisible wall that marathon runners talk of, that place where the future seems too frightening. This is the place where fatigue comes calling. The notion to quit becomes an unwelcome ally, and laying down, for the first time, feels good.

I felt tears running down my cheeks as I realized I was about to let go of everything I'd ever held dear. I leaned back and looked skyward and asked my Heavenly Father to help me sort things out. It was then, my eyes were drawn to the cherry trees, and a revelation began to occur that I'll never forget for the rest of my life.

All morning I'd been cussing those thorns. All morning I'd been wincing from my inconvenience and dabbing the blood from my arms. All morning I'd been missing my wife and worried about my children. All morning I'd been struggling mentally with the financial bind I was currently in. First I was walking, then I was leaning, then crouching, and finally crawling to a place where I was forced to stop.

All of us have come to a point in time when we are forced to look at the bigger picture. Circumstances in life can be unfair and brutal. Maybe it's drug addiction or alcoholism. Maybe it's divorce or rejection. It could be abuse or poverty. For some it's sickness or incapacitation.

These are the thorns of life. They seek to take away your peace and joy. They rob you of your resilience. They take away your self-esteem and threaten your integrity. They can make your dreams seem fleeting and unattainable. They can even cause you to die in the arms of loneliness and despair.

But there is also fruit among those thorns. Many times it is vague and difficult to distinguish, but it's there. It's important not to pass by an apple tree in your hurry to get back into the fray. Try to look beyond the obvious. Look for the deeper meaning. Learn to look hard for the fruit of the spirit.

Often your solutions are just above your head as you lean into your burden and look at the ground as you drag your weight along. The cherry trees taught me to look higher for my answers, for they were there at my reach. As I moved away from the valley and stepped back to look at the whole situation, I was able to see many fruit trees and I was no longer consumed by the thorns and thistles. As I looked deeper into the landscape, I also saw serviceberry, chokecherry, snowberry, mulberry, and currants. I no longer saw the blackberry bushes as an impenetrable bramble of stingy, curved thorns. I carefully pulled them from their purchase by the hundreds until my fingers were stained purple with their juice. Their blood instead of mine—good trade, don't you think?

There was another lesson I learned in the valley that day. Sometimes a person views everything that doesn't hurt him as beneficial. If I would have excitedly run from one berry to another, I could have made a drastic mistake, because there were four additional elements in the bottom that morning: poison oak, hemlock, teasel, and night shade. Getting involved with two of those will make your life definitely uncomfortable, and the other two will kill you.

I no longer viewed my life as a steady string of losses and failures. I happily recalled my love for my wife and the many years we spent together. I thought of my children and what joy it brings me to see them first thing in the morning and the last thing at night.

To know they think of me as the best dad out there is like a cherry tree permanently placed over my head, there for me to touch, to taste, and to enjoy the rest of my life.

I thought of the respect I have from my peers, and the many accomplishments I've made. Suddenly I was bold enough to look to the future, and suddenly I was on my way again. I climbed a thousand feet or so to a small ridge above the valley and decided to wait there until the dogs and I could hook up and go on with the walk. I felt like walking now.

As I casually studied the valley once more, I was fairly amused by what I saw. From this vantage point, I could easily measure the scope of my lesson. From here the fruit trees were dominant. I had to look close to see the thistles, and even the hawthorne looked insecure and insignificant.

It looked like it would be a while until the dogs rejoined me, so I sat down on a rock and began to think. An old story came to my mind, something that had happened to me over twenty years ago, and I was struck by the similarities in this old story and my experience that day.

My endless search for meaning and understanding brought me to a small non-denominational church in Glenwood Springs, Colorado, one Sunday morning. The congregation was small, I'd say fifty or so people, and they met in a remodeled house three times a week.

I didn't really know anyone there, so I found a seat in the rear pew. I didn't want to stick out at the newcomer, and I naturally wanted some degree of separation from the rest of the folks.

Just after I got sat down, I noticed a girl coming through the front door. No one else seemed to be drawn to her, but I had to be staring as she walked through the room looking for a place to sit down.

This girl seemed to be in her mid-twenties, but it was awfully hard to tell based on the condition she was in. She was terribly overweight and she was wearing a dirty sack-type cotton dress that hadn't been washed any time recently. Her shoulder-length hair hung straight and greasy. She was wearing wire-frame glasses that had been broken and taped so many times that they bent around her nose and fairly plastered up against her face. I still have a hard time saying it, but she was the ugliest person I'd ever seen.

She kept moving past the rows of filled pews, and suddenly I looked down beside me at the only empty seat left in the room. Remember, I was the one who wanted separation. I felt a little panic at the thought of losing the distance I had put between myself and the others, but she spied the vacancy and pushed her way into the row beside me. I had made two tactical errors that morning. Number one, I left the space in the first place, and number two, I didn't leave enough room for someone that big. Rolls of fat pushed against my shoulder, and as I scooted over to allow her more room, I noticed that her sleeveless dress bagged way low under her armpits, revealing a dirty, perspiration-stained bra.

She smelled kind of like old tennis shoes. That was the last thing I remembered of that first service. I was so offended because of my unfortunate situation. I didn't hear a word the old preacher said, and the minute he said "Amen," I was out of there like I was shot out of a gun. "How in the world could anyone let themselves go that badly?" I asked myself. I hoped no one recognized me sitting there beside her.

I'm not sure why, but the very next Sunday I found myself driving into the parking lot of that church. I mean, what's the chances of something like that happening again? I scanned the room for her as I walked in, and after being satisfied that she was nowhere to be seen, I settled into the same seat and started glancing through the handout I'd been given at the door. All of the sudden a sense of dread came over me, and I peeked up in time to see the same girl, in the same dress, making her way toward me down the aisle. I know it's unheard of to cuss in church, but that's what I was doing, under my breath, of course.

Sure enough, she plopped down right beside me. Sure enough, she hadn't taken a bath or washed her clothes during the week, and I sat there anxiously until the tennis shoes smell came calling to complete the picture.

I was trying desperately to fight off the feelings that were rampaging through my mind. After all, who was I to pass judgement on someone else? What business of mine was it if she came in there stark naked?

It turned out there was a terrific singing group at that church. They weren't really a choir; they were more of a stage act. They must have practiced endlessly, because their harmony was very tight and they were accompanied by several class musicians.

That group offered me some relief, because my pew-mate was a regular member. They would sing several songs at the start of the service before rejoining the congregation. She would get up to sing and then make her way back to my side for the remainder of the service. I think it was that singing group alone that kept me coming back week after week, even though week after week I found myself sitting by you-know-who.

On the third Sunday she introduced herself.

"Hello, my name's Kathy," she said. "Mine's Mike Gould," I responded.

I guess it was about the fourth Sunday when I started noticing a single voice in the group that was far more refined than the rest. This was the voice of an angel, one of the very best singing voices I've ever heard, before or since.

I started watching their lips so I could discover which one of them possessed this rare gift. I couldn't really decide that day. Maybe it was the pretty girl in the first row with the long dark hair. Maybe it was the preacher's wife—she certainly had an air of confidence up there.

When Kathy came back to jar the wooden pew after the music was over, I said, "Nice job."

"Thank you," she said sweetly. "I still get so nervous singing in public."

The next Sunday I renewed my quest to locate the voice I dreamed about during the week. It had to be the girl with the long dark hair, it just had to be. I listened and watched intently until I matched the voice with the girl. I couldn't believe my eyes at first. It was Kathy. My God, it was Kathy.

An overwhelming feeling of guilt came over me. I felt like an absolute stiff. I had judged her so unfairly. I had already decided there was nothing beautiful about this wretched person, nothing redeemable.

As soon as they finished their last song, Kathy started waddling my way, and I jumped up to meet her. I put my arms around her, well, at least I tried to, and told her how much I appreciated her effort. I looked her in the eyes and told her how sorry I was for my attitude. "Please forgive me, Kathy," I said. "God, I'm such a jerk."

"Oh, that's okay, Mike," she said. "I guess I couldn't blame you, after all. What's to forgive, anyway?"

"Don't you dare let me off the hook that easy. I wish you would just punch me in the face, or get up in front of everyone and tell them what a self-centered dirtbag I am. Maybe you could drag me into the parking lot and beat me to a pulp."

She started laughing, and she wasn't ugly to me any more. Come to think of it, I never saw her through the same eyes again. I came to enjoy her, first through her voice and then as I got to know the person inside. You see, a voice like that can only come through a beautiful heart.

Sometimes I would close my eyes while she was singing, and I could visualize a fashion model with long tan legs and flowing hair. Her greasy, pock-marked face was renewed with smooth, soft skin, and her teeth were straight and as white as snow. From that point on, I was disappointed if Kathy didn't sit by me. Sometimes I would think about buying her a new dress or having her glasses fixed, but I made up my mind never to cross that line again.

I don't know why Kathy never took a bath. I have no idea why she never washed her dress, or her bra. I sometimes wished I could have seen her hair clean and shiny, just once.

I never saw Kathy after that summer, but if the good Lord sees fit to overlook my obvious faults and lets me into his presence, I will be looking for one special angel and one special voice. If He doesn't give her a pretty face and a nice figure in Heaven, He and I are going to have it out. I can only hope she will allow me to sit beside her and to hear her sing is something I dream about.

The midday sun had sweat pouring off me in sheets as I stood to greet my dogs. They had back-tracked down through the ravine and followed me up the hill to the ridge. They were worried about my state of mind, and cocked their heads to look at me. They were inquiring if I was going to be alright.

"Oh, don't get all sentimental on me, you guys," I reassured them. "We've still got a long way to go, and I don't want you two shutting down and blaming me for it."

We swung to the east and cut between wheat and barley fields so we could once again jump out into the big country. The canyon wall was too hot to deal with now, so we headed for the cooler climes of the north slope. Walking across the top felt good to me after knocking it out down in that gorge for most of the morning.

I was still rubbing sore spots and counting scratches.

I pulled my chaps off and tied them around my waist and tucked my gloves under my belt. We reached the northern rim and stopped to look down at a wide, deep drainage of mostly green deciduous trees. My lessons of the morning were still bright in my memory, and I suddenly realized that I was looking at plum trees—thousands of them. Some were yellow, some were red, and some were purple, but they were all plums. Oh, there was an occasional apple tree in the mix, and a hawthorne or two, but literally thousands of plum trees in every direction.

Now I knew it wasn't enough to recognize the fruit amongst the thorns. You must keep moving. You have to keep trying, keep pushing on. If you stay at your task and never give up, someday you will stand in full view of the reward for your effort.

I decided not to go into the drainage that day. I had too much to think about. I had too much to be grateful for. I'm so lucky to have lived the life I have. I have walked where few people have walked before me. I married the only girl I truly loved, and I have four children who bring delight to my every moment.

I have been to the field with thousands of bird dogs and have been formally accepted into the brotherhood of all living things. I have felt the uncommon honor of a few great friends. My own personal record of accomplishments is only complete in the knowledge that I hold no anger or resentment toward any man.

Yes, I've visited the valley, as each of you have, and I've been struck down by the thorns of life. But if you're looking for me, then look to the mountaintop, for it's there you will find me.

If you see the smoke from my fire, you are welcome to sit and share a cup. You will find a caring word, an outstretched hand, and a chain gang full of sure-enough bird dogs who are hard to beat.

"Let's get to the house," I called to the dogs. "We'll come over here tomorrow, eat some plums, and see what that draw has to offer."

We did just that, too, for the following two months. Just think of it—I finally ended up with a job where I can go out to breakfast every morning and still make it to work on time. Things are definitely looking up.

Where You've Been

Run to the nearest mountain top
Above the place where others stop.
Where better living can't justify
The loss of nature from your eyes.
Stop now and look down
At the man-scarred valleys
That seem to frown.
Face the sky and address the human race
Invite them all to this unmarked place.
Where the wind touches your face with
The soft aggressiveness of the sweetest kiss.
Where the reality, the beauty of nature is
Beyond all human comprehension.
Go there
Live there
Learn there
And grow there
Now go back to society, as you must
But with an open heart, full of trust
That the emptiness you live within
Might someday equal where you've been.